Sandstorms And Deals

Donald Trump's Middle East Gamble

GEW Intelligence Unit

Global East-West, London

Contents

1

Introduction

The Return of Donald Trump and the Middle East

Contextualising Trump's Foreign Policy Legacy

The policies implemented by Trump's administration regarding the Middle East region had and continue to have the deepest impact on its geopolitics. His presidency came with new US policies that reconfigured relationships and recalibrated strategic calculations. One enduring element of Trump's foreign policy was his emphasis on transactional diplomacy, which focuses on receiving something in exchange rather than forging alliances or multilateral partnerships. This approach resulted in both advantages and challenges for America's engagement with the Middle East. His administration moved the embassy to Jerusalem, withdrew from the Iran Deal, and held steadfast to pressure policies against Iran while also reaffirming support for Gulf allies, all of which antagonised the region further. The administration's focus on fighting Iran's influence by bolstering support for Gulf allies underscored the maximum pressure strategy, a policy of increasing economic and diplomatic pressure on Iran to force it to renegotiate a new nuclear deal. The Abraham Accords also marked a shift in the focus of peace efforts towards Israel-Arab state normalisation instead of peace for Israel, further transforming regional alignments. These policies also marked a greater emphasis of economic interests on foreign policy, which was a clear shift from previous administrations' balances.

Trump's legacy in the Middle East has ushered in a new era of military policies and partnerships. The shift in perceived security responsibilities and the prioritisation of national interests led to a reduction in troop presence in the region. This realignment tempered the maintained perception of support from other countries deemed as allies. The movement of American forces demonstrated a shift in the reasoning behind strategy to what is termed "national interest". It remains crucial to evaluate the legacy of Trump's foreign policy in light of geopolitical competition and regional context. The intersection of these strategic choices concerning historical tensions and relationships creates alliances ripe for scrutiny. In light of evolving circumstances, the Trump administration's foreign policy defines America's long-term strategy and focus in the Middle East, necessitating a nuanced and comprehensive analysis.

The Middle East Before Trump: A Brief Overview

The Middle East has remained an area of multifaceted geopolitical challenges with deep-rooted historical intricacies. In the 20th and early 21st centuries, the Middle East underwent a sequence of defining shifts and paradigm-changing events that intensified its politics, economics, and security. Since the dissolution of the

Ottoman Empire, followed by the mandate system and the later emergence of independent nation-states, the region has observed a constant state of flux. The Middle East has been profoundly affected by the Arab-Israeli conflict and the rise of political Islam alongside external interventions. Even before Donald Trump became President, the region dealt with many issues, including internecine wars, socio-political power struggles, and economic inequality conflicts. Other regional factors included the Iranian nuclear programme, Syria's civil war, and extremism from ISIS. Equally, long-lasting Israeli-Palestinian tensions have continued to occur in international focus and fuel these conflicts. All these factors have led the region into a highly volatile geopolitical scenario. Alongside these issues, evolving geopolitical conditions have led to a reappraisal of traditional partnerships and alliances.

Prior to Donald Trump taking office, the Middle East had been historically a melting pot of long-standing legacies alongside current conflicts, rivalries, and issues of strategic interest globally. Understanding the historical context is crucial to grasping the depth of the region's complexities and how they became the main focus of US policies during Trump's presidency. This understanding also helps in identifying potential threats that could arise with his return to politics.

Anticipating Trump's Return: Political Landscape Analysis

Anticipation of Trump's return to the political stage has generated significant speculation and analysis, especially about the Middle East. To understand the implications, one must consider the region's political landscape. One such area to focus on is the prevailing power relations or rivalries and their existing alliances, as well as the ongoing obstacles and emerging opportunities that will impact policy choices in the future. This also requires mapping out other significant players and their regional and international goals. Given the peculiar nature of Trump's diplomacy and the lasting consequences of his Administration on the region, the forecast of his return certainly distorts the more nuanced aspects of the region's analysis. Circumscribing the potential consequences of his reemergence needs careful consideration of the multifaceted interactions of the region's concerns, global contexts, and domestic politics. A critical dimension of the expectation also includes determining the degree of engagement of different stakeholders with Trump's policies on the Middle East. Constructing a complete picture from the position of other allies, rivals, and other relevant actors becomes equally important.

In addition to other factors, the impact of changes in the global environment, the increasing activity of other superpowers, and the development of multilateral systems add another level of scrutiny to the analysis. Political landscape analysis remains one of the most important constituents for predicting the possible outcomes and consequences of Trump's return to the Middle East because of its multifaceted nature. It explains why outside powers contest the region, the key interests and conflicts, and what policies need to be adopted to explain important new developments for the region, which is highly relevant for decision-makers, analysts, and regional watchers.

Changing Geopolitical Dynamics in the Middle East

The Middle Eastern region has always exhibited complex geopolitical characteristics due to the ongoing competition for power and influence. Recently, factors of more significant importance have changed the region's stability and security threats across the globe. One of those factors is the traditional partnerships that were previously formed, which are now undergoing some changes. The US managed to broker normalisation talks between Israel and some individual Arab countries, which are now referred to as the Abraham Accords. These new alignments indicate a shift of focus of these countries towards pursuing some new arrangements. This has fundamentally transformed the existing balance of power, undermining old perceptions of regional competition and cooperation. This, coupled with the chronic wars of Syria, Yemen, and Libya, gives the Middle East its current geopolitical character. Another equally important reason focuses on the role of energy resources in the international region. Some shifts in the political and economic dynamics of the global order due to changes in technology and the current demand for energy resources have transformed deep-seated notions about the reason for the existing energy resources' geopolitical conditions within the region.

In addition, non-state actors have contributed to complex problems with their proxy wars and terrorist activities. These problems extend beyond national boundaries and pose severe challenges to local order. At the same time, the Middle East is undergoing profound changes and is beset with multiple security and diplomatic problems. The interplay of state and non-state actors attempts to defend their posture and control the situation while placing sharply contrasting interests and agendas on the negotiation table. It is, therefore, crucial to understand the balance of these conflicting forces to develop reasonable policy options for fostering peace and reducing violence. We tackle these issues head-on, along with a detailed examination of the shifting geopolitical landscape of the region and its impact on the world.

Key Challenges: Security and Diplomacy

One of the global issues of the last few decades has been the intricate web of diplomatic tensions and canny security challenges within the Middle East. Syria, Yemen, and Libya are all hot conflict zones, each with quarrels of their own, and the continuous terrorism threat is nothing but a royal pain courtesy of ISIS and dozens of other militant organisations. Moreover, the advanced militarised equipment, such as ballistic missiles and military drones, further scramble the already overwhelming security puzzle in the region. Not only this, the eternal subsections of Arab rivalries make the whole situation more difficult: the Iranian crisis with Gulf Arab countries and the problem of Palestine and Israel, which has no solution to nowhere. Any attempt to resolve these becomes the merciless target of domination. Western waning empires perpetuate the need to manage these declining power shifts in the exceptionally overwhelming mix of delays, posing a force challenging to master. Located behind the fury is the unmoving force of Iranian nuclear capabilities intertwined with daunting energy issues combined to form the womb of amazing complex geopolitical competition and a keen intervention-diplomatic world. All this means that those compromises and alliances with old friends and new rival businessmen require real mastery from trusted partners on the world stage in Russia and China.

Moreover, resolving chronic conflicts and crafting sustainable peace accords requires novel diplomatic approaches and, at times, excessive attention. The Israeli-Palestinian conflict remains one of the most difficult and multifaceted problems in world diplomacy owing to its ancient history and intertwined narratives of land and sovereignty. These intricate military and diplomatic policy factors require multifaceted solutions that measure directed diplomatic flexibility and military force alongside ongoing international collaboration. The United States must carefully manoeuvre this complex interplay of strategy, historically sensitive terrain, culture, politics, and history to pursue its national objectives within the area. Not tackling these difficulties most efficiently could deeply impact the geopolitical balance of the region and international order, prompting the need for careful analysis and an agile response to the blend of conflicts and threats characterising Middle Eastern diplomacy and security.

Opportunities for Influence: Strategic Interests

The Middle East, a region of profound strategic importance to the United States, presents a complex landscape of challenges and opportunities. The integration of American economic and military power necessitates dominance or influence over stable and secure global regions. A direct policy focus on the Middle East reveals that American objectives in the region revolve around achieving stability, security, and dominance or assertive presence.

The American foreign policy lens indicates a rich opportunity in continuing relations with Israel, Saudi Arabia, and the Gulf states. These allies serve crucial economic and military partnerships and are bulwarks against shared regional rivals. American exertion of influence in accentuating stable and progressive democracies and during notable local skirmishes and wars advances their strategic purpose.

Furthermore, the current energy relations in the Middle East offer another possibility for American expansion of influence. As this region is one of the world's major energy suppliers, the United States is directly interested in ensuring steady and secure activity in the energy market. By interacting with the region's key energy producers and consumers, the United States is working to prevent serious global disruptions and economic downturns, which, in turn, protects its strategic economic interests.

Alongside traditional energy partnerships, the Middle East's changing geopolitical environment provides openings to the US. This region is undergoing shifts in alliances with emerging power dynamics and diplomatic overtures. The US can proactively utilise new partners while reassessing other established relationships to further adapt to change and optimise interests.

Also, promoting democratic ideals, human rights, and economic growth is an example of how the US can positively impact the Middle East. Supporting causes that enhance the level of political and economic opportunities available for skilled citizens propelled by the US will serve American values while also serving important long-term objectives.

The Middle East is complex, multifaceted, and intricately nuanced. Any attempt to understand and leverage opportunities related to this region requires disciplined diplomacy and a refined understanding of relations and interests. However, with a clear strategy outlining its interests, the US can align its goals and play a central role in forging beneficial developments in the region.

American Domestic Politics and the Middle East Policy

How American domestic politics correspond to foreign policy, especially concerning the Middle East, is of utter significance to international relations. The political climate in the US has always framed its policy toward the Middle East, with the region often seen as a theatre for superpower competition. The issue within American domestic politics concerning the Middle East policy requires further scrutiny on the multis of in-depth analysis. In this case, the interest groups, pro-Israel lobbies, energy proponents, and even human rights groups are crucial. These groups have set up expressed interests that enable them to influence American foreign policy through campaign funding, lobby work, and coalitions.

Furthermore, American perception of the Middle East and public image of the conflicts are shaped by the media and can impact the focus and importance given to it. How the confrontations, friendships, and diplomatic relations are presented can have a distinct effect on the decisions taken by Americans in charge. On the other hand, the policy's strategic aspects relating to civilian aspects such as security, trade, or energy also merge international politics with domestic affairs.

In this way, each presidential administration has to find a way to balance these intricate geostrategic relations threads with the country's national interests. Understanding the effects of the Iraq War on public perceptions and the pro-Israeli lobby's impact on US policies regarding Israel and Palestine underscores the significance of the domestic politics intertwining with Middle East policy. The partisanship that characterises the American politi-cal landscape also makes it more difficult to formulate coherent and uniform policies regarding the region. The policies of Middle Eastern countries fluctuate in response to changes in the politi-cal party that exercises control over these countries. Hence, there is little consistency within a firm foreign policy framework. The resulting volatile dynamics are consequential for regional stability and alliances and for enduring strategic objectives.

Moreover, the varying degrees of American idealism, from in-terventionism to outright isolationism, mean that policy debates concerning the Middle East are multifaceted. Integrating these di-verse frameworks and American national interests requires skilful diplomacy and exquisite leadership abilities. Therefore, disentan-gling the complexities of US interests in the region and under-standing the consequences of America's domestic affairs can help provide insight into Middle East policies.

Global Reactions: Allies and Adversaries

Throughout the world, allies and adversaries have had different re-actions following Donald Trump's return to the US political stage. Analysing these reactions is important to understand the conse-quences of a second Trump presidency on international geopol-itics considering the Middle Eastern region. Allied countries in the area like Israel and Saudi Arabia have shown feelings of mixed excitement and hope. These nations enjoyed a close relationship with Trump while in office in his first term due to common wor-ries regarding Iran's expansionist policies and a need to strength-en international trade relations. The expected change back to a more forceful and deal-oriented US foreign policy, which some analysts expected would realign with these countries' interests, was positively received by certain factions. Conversely, more traditional adversaries of the US, such as Iran and non-state actors like Hezbollah and Hamas, have uneasily voiced worries about a possible resurgent Trump administration. The region may be influenced by harsh sanctions, such as those imposed on Iran, and the region-changing international agreements, like the Abraham Accords, set during Trump's first term.

Moreover, their European allies, alongside global watchers like China and Russia, are recalibrating their regional influence and geopolitical strategies considering the possible re-emergence of a Trump presidency. While, in theory, standing with the US as most European countries do, Europe has historically parted ways when it comes to the Middle East, including the Israel-Palestine relationship and Iran. The combination of fractious U.S.-Europe relations with Trump's preceding term resulted in a scenario of deep uncertainty for European allies. China and Russia, who possess their own competing strategic interests in the Middle East, have in the past shifted the focus of their policies to alleviate the possible impacts of Trump's policies. As a result, any changes that suggest a realignment of US policies might force them to revise their strategies at a moment's notice. The rather intricate web of reactions to single-policy changes underscores the need for more nuanced foreign policy strategies focused on the Middle East, and why global relations need to be viewed as one intertwined matrix.

Comparative Frames: Biden vs. Trump

There is an interesting difference in relation to the foreign policy focus on the Middle East between the foreign policies of current President Joe Biden and former President Donald Trump. Both of these individuals have fundamentally changed their attitudes, approaches, and focus areas, which have created and will create certain path dependencies and legacies in this region.

The businessman mentality of the president during Trump's presidency changed the dial of diplomacy and brought about major shifts in the politics of the Middle East. His pulling out of the Iran Nuclear Deal and his zealous support of the Abraham Accords made it clear that his confrontation with Iran would not allow any deals to be made and instead focus on new alliances. Moreover, his policies fostered relationships with a few Middle Eastern countries, more specifically Israel and Saudi Arabia, which is an out-of-the-box tilt from America's longstanding policies.

Unlike Biden, who has sought to mend relations with allies after the Trump administration through diplomacy and a multilateral approach, re-engaging with international institutions and prioritising diplomacy as conflict resolution suggests a shift from the aggressive diplomacy approach of his predecessor. Equally important, there is a striking shift in rhetoric with a commitment to human rights and democratic values in the foreign policy of the Biden administration.

Arguably, one of the most notable continuing legacies of the two contrasting administrations is their differing positions on the Israeli-Palestinian conflict. While maintaining a pro-Israel stance and supporting its government's expansionist policies, Trump granted unconditional support. On the other side of the policy spectrum, Biden has signalled a willingness to restore funding for aid to Palestinians alongside support for the two-state solution, which clearly indicates a departure from the previous administration's nadir policy.

Moreover, each president's approach to the Iranian regime has differed distinctly. With the withdrawal from multilateral agreements, Trump advanced a pressure campaign of economic sanctions, while Biden attempted to re-enter diplomatic discussions with the use of sanctions still in place. These divergent approaches highlight differing underlying beliefs regarding the effectiveness of diplomatic engagement and coercive measures.

Thus, the difference in approaches taken by the Trump and Biden administrations concerning the Middle East offers a striking example of the dynamics of American international relations and the strategies employed for achieving regional equilibrium. By analysing these two approaches, it is possible to gain insight into the complexity of American interventions in the Middle East and the foreseen and unforeseen consequences they may have in the future.

Objectives and Limitations Moving Forward

While studying American foreign policy with a particular focus on the Middle East, it is critical to set specific goals and constraints that have the potential to guide policymakers in strategising future steps. Post-Biden and Trump administrations, there is a complicated puzzle of sustaining equilibrium in the region, ensuring national security, maintaining global coalitions, and addressing the distinct features of the Middle East.

One key priority going forward will be to re-engage with strategically important allies such as Israel, Saudi Arabia, and the United Arab Emirates in a manner that fosters proactive engagement. At the same time, the new administration will have to navigate toward diplomatic warmongering strategies while being mindful of the historically entrenched wounds that sensitive power dynamics geopolitically shaped the region.

In addition, a nuanced approach to regional conflict complexities, especially the Israeli-Palestinian conflict and Iran's ongoing proxy wars, is essential to advancing US strategic interests in the Middle East. The balancing act is to promote diverging interests, human rights, and democratic ideals and restrain destabilising actions without overcommitting or reverting to unilateralism.

These optimistic goals, however, are restrained by inherent limitations: firstly, the conflated regional disputes and the presence of external powers. Acknowledging these limitations requires a responsible approach to policy that seeks to maximise restricted goals with minimal consequences. This approach requires a careful recalibration of the United States' role in the Middle East based on multilateral frameworks and an intricate understanding of the region.

Furthermore, the changing energy system and its relevance to the geopolitical context of the Middle East have both positive and negative implications for US policy. How America balances the need for energy independence with relations to allies and the global market's needs will remain critical to the strategic calculus going forward.

Within these ambitions and constraints, the US must have a holistic, forward-looking strategy beyond domestic political divides and individual leaders. Strong bipartisan agreement and support across international borders will be essential to dealing with the many challenges and opportunities in the constantly shifting Middle East landscape.

2

Evaluating Trump's First Term

Foundation for a Second Gamble

Overview of Middle East Policy Objectives

During his first term, the Trump administration proactively developed and deepened strategic alliances in the Middle East, significantly impacting the region and American interests. From strengthening relations with traditional partners such as Israel and Saudi Arabia to nurturing ties with regional epicentres of power like the United Arab Emirates, the focus was on working with key players for synergistic aims. The United States sought to improve stability, malign force containment, and enhance economic growth in the region. The section highlights the various alliances that were constructed and the mechanisms designed to use these alliances to further US interests in the region, while also analysing the results and studying the challenges and impacts of these actions.

Strategic Alliances Formed and Strengthened

The United States, during Donald Trump's first term, focused on developing and strengthening Middle Eastern strategic partnerships. The administration sought to reinforce existing partnerships while also forming new ones to address emerging problems in the region. A key success of this policy was the expansion of the Abraham Accords, a milestone in changing diplomatic relations in the region. The normalisation agreements between Israel and a number of Arab countries not only recalibrated the balance of power in the region but also enhanced collaboration between former enemies, offering a promising outlook for future diplomatic relations in the Middle East.

In addition to the Abraham Accords, the Trump presidency emphasised strengthening the existing alliances with Saudi Arabia, the United Arab Emirates, and Israel. This included maintaining security support and broadening the scope of economic relations and cooperation on security issues. The administration's strategy to forge a coalition of allies to counter shared threats and aid in stabilising the Middle East was noteworthy.

Apart from the customary interstate engagements, the administration tried to forge relationships with non-state entities, especially regarding security and counterterrorism. Relations with prominent regional actors such as the Gulf Cooperation Council (GCC) and Jordan members highlighted the administration's commitment to common security goals and regional stabilisation. The partnerships' ramifications were felt in diverse areas such as military, diplomatic, and business relations. These newly forged strategic partnerships gave America greater regional control and, at the same time, helped create economically advantageous conditions for several countries, increasing mutual prosperity. These partnerships further acted as pillars to solve the region's difficulties, which included restraining Iran's aggressive expansionism, terrorism, and other forms of extremism.

Still, the first-term alliances had their controversies and critics. Some of the most contested aspects revolved around the lack of multilateral relationships over certain already existing one-sided relationships focusing on human rights issues. Like many other unilateral movements, the emphasis on transaction-focused alliance building was heavily criticised for the longevity of the partnerships formed.

When the possibility of a second term approached, the question of continuity and change came to the forefront concerning the strategic alliances the administration had formed. There was much speculation and debate regarding how the alliances made during the first term would be modified and used by the changing regional realities and new tensions.

Shifts in Military Strategy and Defense Posture

The Middle East has long been at the heart of one of the regions where the United States has focused their attention on military strategy and defence posture, which was even more pronounced during Trump's presidency. One of the pointed shifts noticed was the recalibration of military presence in the region alongside an increased emphasis on burden-sharing. This was partly due to the administration's "America First" doctrine, which sought to curtail US foreign entanglements by subsidising regional allies to become more proactive in their defence. There was realignment in the deployment and basing arrangements of troops to efficiently consolidate resources and reshape commitments. In addition, the administration attempted to embrace new technologies and asymmetric warfare to contend with emerging threats in the region. There was an attempt to adapt to emerging security challenges by developing and deploying new missile defence systems, cyber warfare capabilities, and advanced military systems. Moreover, the previously available blanket approach towards military action was replaced with a more selective and deliberate one, characterised by the strategic use of airstrikes and limited military strikes to signal the new approach.

In addition, the Trump administration changed its arms sales policies, paying special attention to the streamlined processes and increased flexibility for transferring defence articles to preeminent partners in the region. This strategy strengthened allied capabilities, fostering coordination and coalition synergy among regional powers. Nonetheless, these shifts in military strategy and defence posture provoked some criticism because of the negative consequences they could provoke, such as increasing regional tensions and arms races. Although the realignment of military forces was intended to achieve economies of scale by reducing costs and long-term spending commitments, it also created the risk of sending inconsistent signals about America's enduring security commitments to its allies. In addition, the selective application of military force intended to avert drawn-out conflicts risked increasing the chance of scope creep and unintended outcomes. The Trump administration's changes in military strategy and defence posture left a layered and complex US policy in the Middle East through the lens of strategic interests where the mix of retrenchment and reinforcement was applied to pursue stability and national security.

Economic Policies and Energy Strategy

The Trump administration's approach to the Middle East region combines economic policies with strategies related to energy, aiming to reshape broader geopolitical and security considerations. The approach emphasises capitalising on the existing US energy dominance, particularly in oil and natural gas production. One of the most remarkable points of the economic policy has been to market American energy exports to step up the energy independence of regional allies and counteract ordinary energy powers in the area. In addition, there are policies constructed to counter any single supplier or route, which strengthens the global energy framework, diversifies the sources of energy, and the routes through which it is supplied. The administration has also focused on using sanctions and trade restrictions as tools of economic statecraft to support policy objectives and fundamentally alter the conduct of regional counterparts.

This has arisen from the enforcement of selective sanctions on businesses that oppose US interests, such as those involved with Iran's nuclear and missile activities. Furthermore, the region's trade relationships with the global economy influenced the decline of China, as the renegotiated agreements and the onset of a trade war with Beijing also had considerable consequences. These efforts stem from a framework designed to advance diplomatic relations and bolster security alliances in the Middle East using economic force. The combination of economic energy strategies under the Trump administration has received bipartisan praise and backlash.

Supporters highlight the intention and boldness displayed, while sceptics question the viability and consequences of such decisions. It is clear that recalibrating the economy while infusing dynamism into it will result in changes in US foreign policy towards the Middle East, and the process change the region's economy and geopolitical positioning unpredictably.

Diplomatic Engagements and Treaties

President Trump's first term came with new diplomatic engagements and treaties with Middle Eastern countries, unlike any other prior presidents. The administration implemented a transactional diplomacy policy where American power was used in international relations when it was beneficial to the United States and American allies. Perhaps the most lauded diplomatic success was the signing of the Abraham Accords in 2020, which normalised relations between Israel with the United Arab Emirates and Bahrain. The significance of this agreement was that it fundamentally changed the geopolitics of the Middle East as it opened doors for further cooperation in trade, security, and even cultural exchange. In addition, during Trump's presidency, he partook in very aggressive negotiations with North Korea with hopes of mitigating the long-lasting nuclear threat from the regime. Though no denuclearisation deal was reached, it was a sign that the government was pursuing nontraditional diplomatic options. Also, during this term, the diplomatic relations of Sudan were changed from a state sponsor of terrorism to simply a terrorist-supporting state. This decision greatly improved international relations with Sudan and boosted economic growth for the African country.

To address the issues related to the Israeli-Palestinian conflicts, the administration introduced a unique peace plan that aimed at reframing negotiation strategies to create pathways toward enduring solutions. Although not all of them received the plan well, it highlighted the administration's proactive approach to dealing with persistent disputes. An additional factor was how diplomatic engagement rethought established partnerships in the region. The administration relentlessly tried to rethink relationships with major regional partners, expecting them to assume more responsibilities for stability and support in other areas of the region. The administration's policies were the sources of significant trouble, but they also inspired some shifts that strengthened coordinated regional efforts.

Most importantly, the administration focused on Iran's aggressive movements and spread of proxy movements, vigorously working to build a coalition that would commit to confronting Iranian destabilising activities. These efforts resulted in an international partnership to protect important trade routes and restrict Iranian hostilities. Overall, the treaties and engagements of the Trump administration were undeniably considered a break from previous practices while being more aggressive and innovative and focusing on realistic results.

Analysis of Sanctions and Economic Pressures

Sanctioning and economically pressuring a state is a strategic necessity for achieving wider geopolitical goals, and it is a major component of Middle Eastern policy under Trump. His administration, with a clear long-term vision, singlehandedly placed sanctions as well as collaborated with other countries to place them, all while working towards achieving different strategies that targeted Iran. The overall goal was to halt the Iranian nuclear programme, restrict support for Iran's militant proxies, and make the regime change its ways.

These sanctions, a part of a comprehensive strategy, came in the form of individualised "targeted" sanctions, as well as economically comprehensive sanctions that hurt entire sections of the Iranian economy. The two-pronged approach was meant to lead to economic damage on the Iranian government but help the wellbeing of the general population. Nonetheless, the entire approach is extremely controversial and hotly debated.

Some humanitarian critics voiced their dissatisfaction with the economic sanctions, stating how they have deepened pro-Iranian suffering without any change in the ruling elite's behaviour. Alongside these problems, there have been challenges enforcing secondary sanctions towards countries that want to defy the U.S. restrictions and do business with Iran. These issues have highlighted the difficulties of using economic coercion as a single tool of diplomacy.

At the same time, pro and anti-sanctions theorists have been deeply analysing whether the sanctions have offered their intended strategic results. Supporters of sanctions strongly believe that Iran's economy has taken a heavy beating while pushing for severely destabilising activities in the region, and its malign hand is forced to come to the negotiating table now. They also believe that constant economic crises can push the Iranian leaders to change foreign policies, at least in the distant future.

Given the differing opinions, a well-rounded understanding of the impact of sanctions is critical. It requires understanding the intersection of economic sanctions, regional stability, and geopolitical competition. Moreover, the measures' unintended consequences and spillover effects on salient actors within the Middle East region must be analysed. As the situation continues to change, understanding the effect of sanctions and economic coercion will be central to understanding the complex structure of Middle Eastern geopolitics.

Criticism and Controversies Faced

Like other regions of the world, the Trump administration's approach to Middle Eastern policy has come under scrutiny and has faced some criticism. One of the points which has created a lot of debates and discussions has been the management of essential relationships in the area. On the one hand, there have been attempts to reinforce relationships with some friends, such as Israel and Saudi Arabia. On the other hand, a lot of damage has been done to relationships with historical partners such as Turkey and Qatar. This shift in strategy has been criticised for destabilising the region and making it difficult to resolve mutual security issues.

Controversy has stemmed from the decision to withdraw from the Iran nuclear deal, which has garnered mixed responses. On the one hand, some critics claim it could worsen the existing violence in the region and reduce the chances for diplomatic resolutions. On the other hand, proponents claim it is crucial to address Iran's activity, which destabilises the region. The withdrawal and new sanctions created harsh splits among international and regional actors, raising concern about the consequences of the 'maximum pressure' campaign on Iran.

Equally, the administration's approach towards the Israeli-Palestinian conflict has been examined. The decision to accept Jerusalem as Israel's capital, coupled with moving the American embassy from Tel Aviv to Jerusalem, drew ire from Palestinians and a significant part of the world. Proponents of the position claimed it was an unprecedented show of strong support by Americans for Israel. At the same time, detractors contend it fuelled extreme violence in an already volatile region and compromised any hopes of a peaceful resolution to the conflict.

Moreover, the interaction of diplomacy with the rest of the administration's policies has raised issues about the coherence and consistency of U.S. strategy in the Middle East. The reliance on short-term profits through transactional approaches has been criticised for causing ambiguity and volatility and eroding American credibility as a reliable partner.

The controversies and debates surrounding the policies indicate that the region is complex and difficult to understand. Trump's approach is controversial. Some see the disorderly approach as a structural correction of American interests. In contrast, others warn about what can go wrong and the unintended consequences that may follow these contentious decisions and actions.

Key Successes and Achievements

During the Trump presidency, there are a number of notable achievements and milestones in Middle Eastern policy. First, the negotiation and implementation of the Abraham Accords stands out as a beacon of hope, allowing Israel to establish diplomatic relations with several Arab countries. The accomplishment not only enhanced the stability of the region but also indicated potential for other areas of cooperation and engagement in the region.

Second, the Saudi government's self-imposed stance towards Iran aligns perfectly with the U.S. administration's campaign against Iran: the "maximum pressure" policy. The terrorism-supporting militias that Iran funds decreased, leading to increased regional security and diminished Iranian negative influence. Strangely, these expectations were more than fulfilled.

In the meantime, the Israeli-Palestinian issue regarding economic development in Palestine prompted the release of the Peace to Prosperity Plan. The response to this plan was mainly rejection, but it attempted to address problems that had existed for decades and to use them as a basis for investing in Palestine to initiate possible future plans and negotiations.

Finally, these strategic relationships not only balanced Iranian hostility but also enhanced U.S. power over the region. This is something these countries did, contrary to popular belief, as the United States openly supported them. The arms deals that can be made through these agreements and the security offered to the monarchies greatly increased their needs. These governments, especially the Saudis, sought protection from Iran's expansionism and paid dearly for protection from aggressive political extremism.

Secondary effects from the U.S.'s energy sector revitalisation and dominance pursuits resulted in a restructuring of the oil market, which broadened the global energy landscape and diminished the power of oil-wealthy competitors in the Middle East. The enemy nations also had to support the U.S.'s economic investment opportunities, which directly backed economic cooperation within the Middle East region.

Moreover, the Middle East underwent a re-establishment of its primary security and stability due to targeted military actions undertaken by the U.S. government against ISIS, which had constrained operational capabilities.

Completing these initiatives successfully has greatly benefitted the United States politically and economically while demonstrating its skilful navigation through the myriad of complex challenges in the Middle East, which has fundamentally altered the region's politics and security.

Challenges and Lessons Learned

Numerous obstacles and useful insights accompany Trump's handling of the Middle East region. One of the most important challenges was addressing the region's historical disputes and fierce hostilities. The Israeli-Palestinian issue, for example, is one of the deeply rooted problems that is very challenging and time-consuming to resolve, and this poses a major difficulty in the attempts to achieve peace. In addition, there is the ongoing difficulty of balancing America's interests while engaging with the regional powers, which requires sophisticated political manoeuvring and diplomacy.

In addition to the above, there is another important challenge: the development of regional antagonism and amity relations. The Middle East region is in constant flux due to the geopolitical environment and the endeavours and intentions of all local and international players. This issue is geopolitically constrained and complicated because of the region's rich history and the multitude of players with differing goals.

Understanding the subtleties of the Israeli-Palestinian conflict, for example, disproportionality, stresses the necessity of mediation and comprehensible intercultural methods that address deeply rooted animosities on both sides. The value of lessons learned from these challenges is profoundly informative enough to contour plans and strategies. Moreover, the circumflex regional alliances claim to focus on the ever-changing nature of world politics in the Middle East, requiring constant change and proactive focus.

This region's distinct blend of economic interests, security challenges, and diplomatic barriers underscores the need to adopt integrative approaches that take advantage of the existing opportunities with a fair balance of relating to and addressing the articulated challenges. The Middle East's integral wisdom should be centred on these guiding principles gained through rigorous undertakings and profound reflections on harsh realities.

Regarding the Second Trump Term

The world grapples with the possible ramifications of Trump returning to office, particularly considering America's stance with the Middle East. As with any new venture, building upon the initial term would require a careful analysis of what has been done in the previous term and what needs to be done moving forward in the region. Policy changes among traditional allies and new emerging partners with unresolved conflict issues and security challenges are a great reconsideration that needs focus. Defining and implementing policy responses becomes very complex due to changing geopolitical realities and regional evolution. Developing a cohesive response to energy dominance, regional economic stability, and military intervention assertiveness is crucial for the United States to secure a better future for the Middle East.

Furthermore, engaging with Iran while trying not to allow the nation to destabilise the region further remains a very sensitive matter that requires a sophisticated solution. The role of transactional diplomacy practised on regional clients and international players needs to be studied carefully to address the need to protect fundamental interests while deliberately ignoring strategic ones.

In addition, crafting credible strategies to address great power rivalry, especially with China and Russia, is crucial to protecting U.S. interests in the Middle East. There is an opportunity to assess the impact of previous policies, which allows a second term to be more flexible and imaginative where change is desirable. The administration can proactively manage unknown challenges and take advantage of new opportunities in the Middle East by integrating the positive outcomes from the first term, acknowledging the negative outcomes, and using the experience from the first term. After all, the ramifications of a second term explain the need for a profound and integrated strategy with a sophisticated blend of diplomacy, vision, and knowledge of the nuanced characteristics of the region.

3

The Abraham Accords

Expansion and Implications

Overview Of The Abraham Accords

The invocation of the Abraham Accords illustrates a new peak in the history of the Middle East, as it transcends boundaries of hate and conflicts entrenched in the territory. It was foremost upheld by the United States, a key player in global politics, which sought to erode hostilities in the Middle Eastern region by normalising ties between Israel, an Arabic nation between the Gulf of Jordan, the UAE and Bahrain. This development also sought promotion through new agreements from other neighbouring countries, with the treaty signed in September 2020. "While hoped for," many analysts along with regionally affiliated citizens of the Middle East deemed this revolutionary 'vision' unprecedented.

The inception of the accords came about because all of the

parties involved had aligned strategically with the economic goals about infringing the security measures. The initiatives governed the need to shift focus towards younger populations and emerging economies within the region succumbing to globalisation. Hence, the Accords embody the drive towards a more innovative and optimistic governance approach in the Middle East focused on improvement and dependency on working "beyond the hallowed narratives of the past." As the advantages accompanying the accords become more attractive, the incentives for adopting them will only increase further.

Moreover, the inauguration of the Abraham Accords stimulated a shift in the shared perception of the Middle East and created a new understanding of possibilities and collaboration within the region. It sparked discourse around the possibility of using collaborative approaches in solving existing regional issues, including utilising available resources and cultivating relations that promote interdependence.

This advancement is significant for the countries that signed it and the rest of the world since it creates opportunities for enhanced interdependence, prosperity, and security.

The multi-angled relationship of the Accords, combining diplomacy, commerce, security, and cultural interaction, illustrates efforts made to form strong, lasting relations. This shows that continued cooperation is only possible if an all-inclusive framework is developed beyond political motivations, taking into account the needs and views of other interested parties.

This is why the Accords remind us of what is possible through historically respectful, understanding, and beneficial relations among nations with differing viewpoints.

In summary, the journey from conflict to cooperation as captured by the Abraham Accords tells a story of enduring resolve, pragmatism, and audacious vision. It remains illustrative of Israel's ability for transformative leadership and its enduring quest for peaceful coexistence. Further scrutiny of the accords reveals that its implications go far beyond any tangible benefits, instead serving as a hopeful symbol of opportunity within a region characterised by chronic tensions and conflicts. The Accords have the potential to transform the Middle East into a region of stability and prosperity.

Historical Context: From Conflict to Cooperation

The major conflicts and geopolitical struggles in the Middle East led to the signing of the Abraham Accords. The Middle East has always been known for its conflicts regarding territories and power battles that occur between different nations. Israel was established as a sovereign state in 1948. This event brought about deep-rooted hostility and wars with its neighbouring Arab countries. Adding fuel to the fire is the Israeli-Palestinian dispute, which, until today, has been considered one of the most controversial conflicts in the world and revolves around competing stories of ownership, violence, and nationalism. The region's landscape is also filled with proxy wars, fights between superpowers, and chaos. The difficulty in understanding the historical context of the Abraham Accords renews hope in these waging disputes. The Accords, on the other hand, mark the first treaties signed by Israel with countries it has fought against and considers as enemies. This is the first step towards peace and is on the way to achieving stable, everlasting peace in the region.

The Accords indicate an ability to set aside historical grievances and diplomatically relate based on common goals towards stability and prosperity. By analysing history, one can appreciate the striking patterns of distrust, lost inflexion points, and deliberative pivots that led to the remarkable achievement of the Abraham Accords. Appreciating the complicated past is equally important in understanding the great gaps of meaning about the evolving diplomacy and collaboration within the region. The diplomatic context is necessary to understand the degree of change this deep-rooted agreement brings and to evaluate the possible ramifications of the accords on the future of the Middle East.

Key Players and Nations Involved

The Abraham Accords are seen as a milestone in foreign policy diplomacy. Several important actors and countries in the Middle East were involved. The main actors were Israel, the United Arab Emirates (UAE), Bahrain, and the United States. All these parties were actively involved in the negotiation, execution, and further development of the Accords.

Israel, a country that has been in conflict for decades, serves as a key participant in the Accords. The Israel UAE accords were signed after Israel committed to normalising relations with the UAE and other Arab states. The shift in relations between the two nations marks a drastic change in long-standing policies in the Arab world. The leading Gulf state, the UAE, showcased its vision by boldly establishing full relations with Israel, becoming the first Arab state to lead the way for other countries.

Bahrain's endorsement highlighted the growing trend toward embracing peace and collaboration in the Middle Eastern region. Alongside these central players, the United States, under President Donald Trump's leadership, provided the needed enthusiasm and backing to the Accords, guiding the negotiations and developing diplomatic initiatives among the parties.

The Accords have already affected many other countries worldwide beyond the primary participants. Oman, Sudan, and Morocco all supported normalising relations, indicating possible new avenues for collaboration. Moreover, superpowers like Russia, China, and some European countries observed closely the changes taking place because of the Saudi-Israel agreements, understanding that much can change the region's stability and global politics.

The reasons for each nation participating in the Accords have uniquely different motives but share a common goal of redefining diplomatic relationships in the Mideast. The motives include accepting Israel regionally, the US realigning their strategies, Gulf states diversifying their regional relationships, and many others. This explains the economic and security complexities involved.

To understand the impact and significant contributions of the emerging powers in the region, it is vital to appreciate the active yet diverse roles of the key countries and actors during the Accords' negotiation and implementation phases.

Diplomatic Strategies and Negotiations

Resolving the conflicts and advancing the nuanced diplomacy related to the Abraham Accords was of strategic importance and required an exceptional blend of skills in intricate diplomacy and complex negotiation. For each participating nation, the start of the negotiations was accompanied by various geopolitical factors and an understanding of each nation's priorities and their level of sensitivity. With careful application of diplomatic tactics, significant actors worked to overcome the entrenched divides and settle notorious divisions to reach productive conversation. Key diplomats had carried out their initiatives in trust building to highlight the possible formation of regional coalitions with the aim of unprecedentedly positive alliances, which could result from achieving mutual respect. There was heavy scepticism and doubt regarding the effectiveness of the negotiations, which was overcome through diplomacy to achieve a paradigmatic change in international relations. Combining multilateral and bilateral strategies, the negotiators sought to solve the conflicting interpretations of dominant forces in history along with competing perspectives and searches for regional solutions. One of the most sensitive and uncharted domains was upholding territorial and sovereign self-governance while attempting to detach from the correlation comforting mediations claimed to put the parties in. Leaving these delicate frameworks was one of the greatest tasks demanding skilful handling alongside conflict resolution. It took careful balancing of momentum, constructive delay tactics, and aggressive navigating of advancing power struggles to resolve conflict.

During the negotiations, it became clear that the strategies considered highlighted the importance of using both hard and soft power approaches in preserving the credibility and strength of the Accords. In this case, economic rewards and mutual security guarantees were emphasised, as pragmatic cooperation and coexistence propositions were sought after. The culmination of the process showed a continuous commitment to peace and prosperity, further enforcing the core belief that conflict is best resolved not through force but via consistent dialogue and negotiations.

Economic Partnerships and Trade Agreements

The creation of economic partnerships and trade agreements marks the significance of the Abraham Accords, especially in its context of moving from historic animosities to cooperation in the region. After diplomatic breakthroughs, concerned countries have sought to develop strong economic relationships to foster growth and interdependence within the Middle Eastern region. The increased availability of trade routes and channels for investment demonstrates a significant shift from historical geopolitical rivalries towards a new era of comradeship. With the advancement of bilateral relations, the concentration on the economic facets of the relations indicates a commitment to sustainable development and common benefits.

A key aspect of the economic dimension of the Abraham Accords is the development of trade agreements that enable the movement of goods and services across borders. The contracting parties aim to establish a framework for enhanced trade and economic growth by removing barriers to trade and aligning their regulatory regimes. These accords facilitate increased market access, heightened import-export activities, and invigorated entrepreneurial initiatives through policy alignment. Furthermore, mutual recognition of each other's comparative advantages gives rise to synergistic economic relations, harnessing the strongest aspects of the participating economies.

In addition, signing economic partnerships extends the scope of trade agreements to include more complex relations involving strategic investment and joint venture agreements. This combination of factors enhances economic activities and promotes the development of international collaboration in many industries, such as technology and innovation, infrastructure, and energy. Nations can be empowered by pooling resources and expertise, which fosters an environment ripe for innovation and sustainable growth. When coupled with the ability to invest in other partnering nations, the joint funding of projects can support the diversification of economies, the advancement of technology, and job creation to strengthen the socio-economic framework of partner nations.

It is clear that the economic relations and trade agreements, under the umbrella of the Abraham Accords, go beyond immediate profits by helping to create long-term regional stability and development. By amalgamating economic factors, the signatory states develop interdependence and mutual benefits that serve the eminent goal of achieving durable peace and security in the Middle East. The development of mutual economic relations accelerates socio-political relations and creates an atmosphere of peace, goodwill, and cooperation. Consequently, the development of economic relations and the resulting interdependence contribute to creating a stable and developed region in the Middle East founded on shared economic interests and mutual cooperation.

Security Collaborations and Regional Stability

The Abraham Accords have brought about a profound transformation in the Middle East's security landscape. By fostering new economic opportunities and initiating cultural exchange, these Accords have not only normalised relations between Israel and other Arab countries but also created a perception of balance of power and collective security in the region. This significant development has sparked discussions on mutual defence pacts, intelligence cooperation, and joint military training exercises among the member states.

These collaborations, a direct result of the Abraham Accords, are a strategic effort to address regional stability by countering common enemies and threats. The primary concern for the participating countries is the Iranian influence and its proxy forces, and the Accords have paved the way for coordinated action to face these challenges. Furthermore, the Accords facilitate greater cooperation in border security and counter-terrorism efforts, thereby enhancing the defence posture of the involved states.

In addition, the normalisation of relations has resulted in discussions on crisis management and conflict resolution mechanisms to lower the chances of unsettling security risks. By developing trust and decentralised communication systems, the nations are working towards a more secure environment that can resist external pressures and internal weaknesses. The cooperative approach to security also covers maritime and navigational safety about key waterways, aligning the collective interests of the countries concerned in protecting essential infrastructure and trade channels.

Furthermore, the repercussions of these security collaborations go beyond immediate bilateral relations, deepening the strategic balance of power in the region. The agreements have set the ground for peaceful coexistence and positive interaction, defying old animosities and facilitating a transition to a more unified security framework in the Middle East. Thus, they provide the basis for confidence-building actions and create an environment for enduring peace and stability.

Nonetheless, it is important to recognise the dynamics and nuances regarding these security partnerships, given their nexus with legacy issues, conflicts of interest, and divergent geopolitical lines. Balancing differences in regional security and other issues turns into a juggling act of competing stakeholders and emerging relationships. In the same way, balancing gaps in military strength with adequate representation in security policies remains an issue that requires great effort and complex problem-solving.

To sum up, the strategic partnerships set up through the Abraham Accords are among the most remarkable shifts in the recently emerging security order of the Middle East. This transformation is expected to follow as the member states increase their interac-

tions and threshold joint frameworks towards cooperative relations. This would enhance regional stability and collective security,
undoubtedly a good omen for the area.

Cultural Exchanges and People-to-People Ties

Cultural exchanges and people-to-people contacts are not just a
formality, but a powerful tool for fostering mutual understanding and lasting peace among nations. The circumstances of the
Abraham Accords provide a fertile ground for such exchanges to
flourish, promoting cultural dialogue, tolerance, and deepening of
values. The acceptance of exchange relations between Israel and
some of the Arab countries has enabled further cultural cooperation, offering more opportunities for the exchange of art, music,
literature, culinary arts, and even traditions. These exchanges act
as transformative tools, enabling people on the ground to change
their perceptions about one another and paving the way for a more
harmonious future.

In addition, introducing non-stop flights and tourism between
the signatories has created more opportunities for citizens of other
countries to interact with people from different cultures and participate in cross-cultural activities. Dance, music, culinary arts, and
tourism to important historical places, religious sites, and lively
modern cities enable people to understand more about their new
partners, making it possible for people to have genuine experiences
while beginning to appreciate each other's culture.

As noted above, collaboration in education has emerged as a key
form of cultural engagement under the framework of the Abraham Accords. This document, along with the other agreements
signed under the Accords, has opened up opportunities for educational collaboration, including student mobility programmes,

academic research, and collaborative projects aimed at acquiring and disseminating knowledge across borders. These initiatives not only promote learning and scholarship across borders but also foster friendships and relationships among future leaders, who will play a crucial role in maintaining the spirit of cooperation and understanding.

Encouraging the learning of Arabic and Hebrew languages and fostering proficiency in them is a crucial step in strengthening the cultural relations among the countries involved in the Abraham Accords. In the context of these countries, language is a powerful connector that allows for communication on different levels, providing a deeper understanding of the people being engaged with. When people learn to speak in each other's languages, they break down barriers and open up avenues for genuine interaction and understanding, thereby strengthening cultural ties and fostering a sense of unity.

Simply put, the development of cultural interactions and people-to-people relations initiated under the Abraham Accords provides a remarkable opportunity to achieve enduring peace and reconciliation in a region notoriously marred by violence. Such undertakings go beyond political conventions and economic pursuits, extending into the land of sentiments where genuine differences and peace flower for the benefit of coming generations.

Perspectives and Reactions from Global Powers

Global actors have followed the progress of the Abraham Accords with a blend of fascination and caution. These agreements yield considerable concern from international stakeholders owing to their value regarding regional conflicts, global power relations, and diplomacy. The growing economic interdependence amongst countries globally is linked to the positive response from global actors. The response is complex, as the instituted diplomatic accords were sought to unlock opportunities within the Middle East as a region alongside grappling powers.

The United States, as the primary designer and negotiator of the Accords, holds a significant position in supporting these agreements as a vital approach towards achieving the desired progression in the area. The Trump-led government initially approached these accords as a dominating concern for addressing power balance politics internationally, and despite shifts in government, these sentiments remain. However, the stance on the accords by the Biden government may become more sophisticated, working with other countries while favouring a unilateral principle concerning normalisation accords.

On the other end of the spectrum, Iran and its partners have expressed their concerns regarding the accords more publicly. Tehran, alongside its allies, has viewed the normalisation of relations between Israel and Arab countries as an annexation of their influence and a challenge to their regional supremacy, thus portraying it as a surrender to Israel's waning interest in Arab unity and betrayal to Palestine. Because of this, they have vehemently condemned the accords for dry and hollowed pan-Arab unity against the advanced Israeli militaristic policies.

At the same time, European countries like France, Germany, and the United Kingdom have leaned towards cautious optimism but tempered it with genuine worries. Considering the Accords might lead to greater stability and economic development for the region, it is still vital that no new superseded Israeli-Palestinian relations obstruct peace talks, especially a two-state solution framed in peace treaties, which are fundamental for a healthy and equal coexistence.

Moreover, regarding the Abraham Accords, Russia and China have balanced stances as leading power holders in global politics. Both have sought to solidify their relations with countries in the region to increase their global influence while strategically countering Western powers' dominance over the Middle East's geopolitics.

The range of international reactions highlights the intricate web of motives and views that surround these momentous diplomatic efforts. As the Accords continue to have effects around the world, the relations and interactions between the major global powers will further influence the direction of the changing geopolitical scenario of the Middle East.

Challenges and Criticisms of the Accords

Much celebrated as a landmark diplomatic achievement, the Abraham Accords have also come under criticism for their lack of inclusivity, particularly towards the Palestinian Authority, raising the question of whether it further exacerbates Palestinian tensions. Concerns have also been raised regarding the potential failure of the Accords to address the core issues of the Israel-Palestinian conflict while simultaneously risking the probability of a sweeping peace treaty. There appears to be further concern about the enduring nature of the Accords in the face of changes in leadership or geopolitical shifts, which sometimes tend to shift the most. Moreover, the inclusion of Israel within the regional framework faces some opposition, as several countries struggle with popular support for normalised relations with the Jewish nation. Furthermore, opposition regarding the internal relations of some Arab states with Israel has been labelled as controversial for its implications for aid to the Palestinian cause. On another note, the Accords' impact on the Middle East's regional power balance is equally concerning. Detractors worry that a shift in alliances will result in the deterioration of fragile alliances and increased international division in the volatile region.

This is especially important in light of the conflicts with Iran and its regional rivals. There has also been controversy regarding the Accords and their impacts on the balance of power in the Middle East, as well as the fears of new volcanic eruptions from reshaped geopolitical dynamics. Some challenges also incorporate economic dimensions, particularly regarding the underlying economic partnerships and trade agreements within the Accords. These conflicts of interest make the arrangement politically sensitive due to animosities rooted both historically and geopolitically. Furthermore, the issue of building and fostering long-lasting reconciliation and peace requires attention. They state that conflict is diagnosed, but the lack of enduring peace and stability for the involved parties is often neglected. That means effectively engaging with key players and strengthening the system is essential to change the status quo in the region. The challenges and criticisms must be constructively addressed to develop a reliable path to enduring peace in the region despite celebrating the transformative realities expected from the Abraham Accords.

Future Outlook: Sustaining Peace and Progress

The Middle East's future looks bright and intricate after the signing of the Accords. Moving forward, as with any global roadmap, all parties need to put in effort alongside avoiding potential risks to fully capture the opportunities given to them. From the looks of things, the Accords have outlined a new pathway to diplomacy and regional cooperation, which will invoke a need to rethink and re-plan strategies for their success.

A crucial consideration in meeting the expectations is the dialogues and interactions between the countries that choose to sign the accords. At first, it should be the main priority to establish dialogue leading to mobilisation; later on, based on the outcomes of these meetings, there can even be regular, face-to-face interactions among the ministers, which leads to other domains such as security, economic growth, and even cultural cooperation. It is also helpful to provide a set of commands and groups for mobilisation so that disputes can be promptly resolved.

The incorporation of civil society and people-to-people initiatives is important in building peace and sustaining a society. Up to this point, the Accords have stemmed from governmental action. The participation of non-profit organisations, schools, and local actions will improve societal relations, foster understanding, and help in public reconciliation processes. Cross-religious dialogue, teaching, and other joint activities will make stronger and more sustainable peace possible.

Trade and other economic activities are also important for the region's future. As such, the Accords could enhance the region's economic progression by focusing on the added value of every participating country in innovation, entrepreneurship, and youth employment. Targeted investment policies for economic zones and business development will lead to increased employment, new technologies, and economic benefits, strengthening the countries' bonds.

Identifying issues about the sustainability of the Accords is important even when considering the available opportunities. Geopolitical considerations, security paradigms regarding the region, and exogenous factors may derail the path the Accords intend to follow. Hence, it will be important to defend against anticipated disruptions while simultaneously taking advantage of the existing synergies and convergences.

As stated above, what lies ahead in the Middle East will be futile without proper guidance. Put forth in clearer terms, the Abraham Accords have integrated peace and development, which together unlock a peaceful measure in the Middle East.

Considering the argument presented, attaining perpetual peace and advancement post the Abraham Accords will be drawn from sustaining a well-thought-out and balancing diplomatic policy with social, economic, and strategic initiatives. Stronger emphasis shall be placed on the vision of collective economic good, shared safety, and intercultural activities anchored within the Accords. This will no doubt lay a more reliable Eastern Mediterranean region, which is anticipated to be passed on through generations.

4

Saudi-Israeli Relations

A New Chapter in Normalisation?

Historical Context and Evolution of Relations

Saudi Arabia and Israel have had a unique relationship that lacks full diplomatic recognition, characterised by a blend of practical coordination and rival-hostile dynamics. Despite the formal absence of contacts, the relations have undergone considerable changes and developments. After analysing the history of these countries and their relationship, it becomes clear that several key events, the aftermath of WWII, the emergence of the state of Israel in 1948, the Arab-Israeli conflicts like the five-year war alongside the six-day war in 1973 shifted the reality of geography profoundly. The development is further exacerbated by the issues of Palestine, the expulsion of Palestinians, and the support of the Arab League towards Palestine while adopting the Khartoum Resolution in 1967.

The Role of the Abraham Accords in Shaping Dynamics

These transformative events also included the formation of the Trump administration, which oversees diplomatic mixing within the Middle East. So, in congruence with the achieved changes, the agreement will allow us to gain further insight into the functioning relations of Israel and Saudi Arabia, fostering new potential further rooted alongside Novosibirsk.

The historic diplomatic achievement resulted in the normalisation of relations between Israel, the United Arab Emirates, and Bahrain. The normalisation process has been vital in changing regional perceptions and alliances, likely having far-reaching consequences in multiple areas. First, the Accords have indicated a remarkable transformation in traditional geopolitical considerations as they marked the departure from the Arab world's unified precondition regarding Israel—the resolution of the Palestinian conflict—as a prerequisite for establishing sustained relations with Israel. This symbolic departure set the stage for others to consider similar gestures towards Israel, thereby upending the status quo and defying prevailing conventions. So, it reframed the extent to which Saudi Arabia and Israel could be imagined in candid discourse and cooperation. The Accords arguably supplied this blend of factors with powerful impetus to be acted upon urgently. From curtailing Iranian assertiveness to enhancing economic collaboration, the Accords focused on shared interests and goals, fostering a convergence of political and strategic pathways for Saudi Arabia and Israel. This shift stands to change the power relations in the region and bring about stability by supplanting deep-seated hostilities. Reduction of historical animosities may transform the regional power dynamics and foster stability. The greatest significance of the Abraham Accords is the change in people's perceptions and attitudes in Saudi Arabia.

The normalisation process has stirred contentious debates and internal discourse around Israel, showcasing a unique combination of deep-seated animosities, sensitive religious nuances, and national identity. While some groups within the nation seem to accept this newfound relationship, others have shown scepticism or outright rejection, highlighting sociopolitical intricacies within the Kingdom. Moreover, the Accords have fuelled considerable international focus and reaction from other international powers and organisations. The measures taken by the United States to support and sponsor these agreements have emphasised the role of outside actors in the affairs of the Middle East. Also, the impact of this shift on enduring local controversies and power structures must be recognised. As Saudi-Israeli relations shift in this direction and grapple with the intermingled dynamics of other great powers, there is a need for careful strategy to seize potential opportunities and minimise emerging difficulties. The hope offered by the Abraham Accords captures the prospect of recalibrating Middle Eastern geopolitics, marking a new shift towards cooperative potential and transforming relations between Saudi Arabia and Israel.

Political and Strategic Interests: A Converging Path

The alignment of Saudi Arabia's political and strategic interests with Israel's impacts the entire Middle East region's geopolitics. In the past, these two states have dealt with complex relationships diverging with sub-region frameworks and ideological narratives. Nonetheless, changing geopolitical realities, security necessities, and realignment of relations have created possibilities of interest alignment beyond traditional animosities.

In the case of Saudi Arabia and Israel, they are both grappling with emerging challenges from regional state actors such as Iran and non-state actors like Hezbollah and Hamas. The need to contain Iran's influence and its ambitions for dominating the region has borne the prospects of cooperation among these countries, who understand the importance of policy synergies. Furthermore, coping with the complex power relations of the Gulf Cooperation Council (GCC) and the Arab World has inflicted revisions to their foreign policy, nurturing a more cynical and pragmatic shift rather than ideologically fixated on doctrine.

On the other hand, more fundamental shared interests centre on concerns regarding the potential for regional destabilisation, terrorism, and developing a unified defence system that protects national interests and strategic regional alliances. The rising concern of transnational threats such as cyber warfare, asymmetric warfare, and even the proliferation of weapons of mass destruction have made it crucial to focus on collaborative approaches in further sharing intelligence, joint exercises, and even technology innovation. In addition, the role of the United States in mediating regional reconciliation and strengthening coalitions against shared enemies has further intensified the need for the synchronisation of strategic objectives.

Both countries are acknowledging the immediate and mid-term security strategies and the economic benefits advanced collaboration could bring. Prospective joint projects in trade integration and infrastructure development and capitalising on comparative advantages in renewables, desalination, and healthcare could foster development and prosperity. Once Saudi-Israeli political relations evolve from mere inter-state conflict to constructive engagement, economic dependence will not only be a driver of deeper ties but will also transform the region's economic environment.

To sum up, Saudi Arabia's and Israel's alignment of geopolitical and strategic interests marks a shift in the dynamics of the Middle East.

With the changing power balances due to intra-regional cooperation and historical rivalries transforming into contemporary competition, a cohesive approach to regional order, development, and well-being is likely to establish a new paradigm in the region for the years to come.

Economic Opportunities and Collaborative Ventures

Driven by the recognition of shared opportunities, Saudi-Israeli relations are changing from diplomatic to practical and economic collaboration. The Saudi Arabia Vision 2030 and Israeli technological entrepreneurship serve as a fertile ground for joint ventures and strategic partnerships. Both nations are in the process of expanding economically, which creates reliance on nontraditional sector industries, and there is a growing awareness that cooperative efforts can provide economic value. Collaboration in renewable energy, water preservation, agriculture, and advanced manufacturing offers the potential to solve common problems and develop sustainably. Moreover, Israeli technological ventures and Saudi Arabian investment abilities are likely to form groundbreaking projects that change the region's economic landscape. This shift in relations has further provided opportunities for trade, investment, and infrastructure development. With both countries actively trying to maximise their strengths, these industries are more likely to succeed: healthcare, cybersecurity, and financial technology. The initiatives provide an economic boost and result in innovative solutions, new employment opportunities, and the outsourcing of knowledge that helps citizens from both sides.

With the growing Saudi-Israeli relations, which include economic interdependence, trade, and investment opportunities, areas for doing business are increasing. These relations are not only bilateral but also regional, making use of the GCC's potential alongside other newly formed relations within the Middle East. Israeli and Saudi relations, if synergised and integrated, can greatly progress, stabilise and enable more advanced geopolitical prosperity.

Security and Defense Cooperation: Shared Imperatives

Saudi-Israeli cooperation on security and defence reflects shared imperatives of concern and strategy focus on achieving certain regional goals. Both countries strongly agree on the need to increase cooperative measures against prevalent non-state and state-sponsored terrorism in the Middle East. The new world order has made it imperative to align these policies to protect and stabilise these interests.

Israel and Saudi Arabia have been increasingly active in searching for ways to cooperate on military drills, intelligence cooperation, and technological development. These efforts are designed to improve their handling of asymmetric warfare, cyber warfare, and ballistic missile proliferation. In addition, negotiating the possible purchase of advanced defence systems and other equipment has been part of the conversations, signalling a readiness to use available expertise and resources to improve defence and security simultaneously.

The combined imperatives go beyond military concerns to encapsulate other aspects of security. Both countries understand the importance of marine security for the Gulf and the Red Sea, where the fight against piracy, smuggling, and other nefarious activities is growing. Border control and guarding important national installations also figure prominently in their cooperative plans to consider the danger of cross-border incursions and attacks.

The need for cooperation in the area of intelligence is imperative under these circumstances. Other alliance members are as heavily engaged in the region and seek to deal with the same threats. The framework includes information sharing, individually and in groups, and evaluating potential and existing threats, constituting a joint response to new security risks. Also included are actions in counter-terrorism and those aimed at stopping the spread of radicalism that encompass the security partnership.

In addition, the debates around integrating security doctrines and operational methods suggest an advanced synergistic undercurrent of deterrence and resiliency strengthening. The dominant shared goals make it imperative to actively attend to the dialogues on strategy, management systems, and risk evaluation, thus enabling evolution in preparedness against new challenges.

Saudi Arabia and Israel are trying to shift their security policies with the new changes in the region, so joint cooperative agreements focus more on resilience, interoperability, and comprehensive preparedness. These frameworks highlight the shared motives of defence and security cooperation, which provide opportunities for further cooperation towards an alliance that enhances the collective security system of the Middle East.

Public Perception and Sociopolitical Challenges

Public sentiment and socio-political difficulties are particularly important regarding Saudi-Israeli relations. Despite considerable diplomatic and economic progress, both sides' societal sentiment and collective history remain an intricate [sociocultural] barrier to complete normalisation. Cultural differences, religious sensitivities, and entrenched animosities have nurtured unshakable prejudices that elicit scepticism and defiance from the people. The perpetuation of these attitudes, both in public life and in public debate, makes cementing the relationship even harder.

Public opinion in Saudi Arabia concerning Israel remains highly polarised. Even with the visible change in the officially sanctioned narrative from the Kingdom, which is attributed to strategic interests and shifting power dynamics in the region, broad segments of society continue to be sceptical and cautious. The decades-long investment in anti-Israeli propaganda, knitting together the Palestinian cause and the regional hegemonic rivalry, has inundated society with deep animosity and suspicion. The royalty, in their foreign policy, is forced to deal with the pragmatic realities of the world while balancing domestic sensitivities by not making any obvious soft proposals to Israel.

The perception of Saudi Arabia in Israel reflects a blend of historical animosity, tempered hope, and realpolitik concerns for security. The divide does not seem to affect the Israeli public's backing of the government, which is eager to reconcile with the Gulf states. However, some segments of the population remain reluctant to embrace former foes. The Israeli perspective seems to be heavily influenced by the memories of the Arab oil embargo and the regional conflicts that have taken a toll over the years. In addition, the socio-political framework is impacted by competing narratives within Israeli society regarding the need to prioritise peace with the region over the preservation of Jewish identity and historic wounds.

To resolve these socio-political hurdles, more scope is needed, including educational programmes, cultural activities, and inter-group communication. These activities change perceptions that portray an individual or group in a negative light and promote understanding of their true attributes. Changing stereotypes is very difficult, but by altering the narrative of partnerships, empathy and experience can be fostered. Tackling these issues head-on can relieve some of the fear and misconceptions surrounding the warming of relations. Striking a balance between these historic grievances and a focus on shared interests can serve as a basis for leaders of both nations to cultivate acceptance of cooperation.

Regional Implications and Global Geopolitical Reactions

In its totality, the Middle East has responded to the normalisation of Saudi-Israeli relations, providing ample material to discuss on a global level. The Saudi-Israeli endeavours have elicited responses, albeit sometimes appearing quite the opposite, from international authorities, ranging from the two states to the EU. As these two countries have developed a mutual understanding, the United States, for example, has heavily sided with the development and is promising new diplomatic efforts in the Middle East, which seem bold at the moment, to further deepen this new relationship. With the Abraham Accords, the US heavily focuses on the Iranian international-diplomatic relationships these two countries share regionally. In stark contrast, African states have provided a different perspective on aid aimed at building new cooperation platforms, claiming that the traditional sense of Arab identity is being greatly neglected in favour of international Arab relations.

The United States, a strong supporter of the new Abraham Accord, has desperately attempted to make this newly formed partnership initiate other negotiations directed towards the Middle East and serve to pull this into the region. It views such diplomacy as a potentially provocative breakthrough in scouting Arabic-strategically cloaked links in situ, which simultaneously acts as a target for Iranian and other Middle Eastern powers.

While observing the responses on both regional and global levels, the developing Saudi-Israeli relationship has triggered discussions concerning the inevitability of the future outlook of other parts of the Middle East. Policymakers and other analysts have speculated on the possibility of a new form of regional synthesis that goes beyond the region's axial rifts while also considering the region's deep-seated conflicts alongside interwoven complexities of history. Therefore, creating this new transformational partnership brings another set of factors to an already complex geopolitical environment, which requires careful manoeuvring and diplomacy.

The US Influence: Encouraging Diplomatic Bridges

As the Middle East undergoes a steady transformation, the United States continues to play a pivotal role in fostering diplomatic relations between long-standing adversaries like Saudi Arabia and Israel. The U.S. has historically been a major player in the Middle East, and its guidance has been instrumental in stabilising dialogue and relations among the nations in the region.

The United States' power to encourage the construction of diplomatic bridges is multifaceted. The US can persistently negotiate diplomatically, fostering relationships, understandings, and trust between Saudi Arabia and Israel. The United States' strategic imperatives have often helped consolidate the aims of bridging these key actors in the region to achieve stability and economic growth in the Middle East.

In addition, the US has seen a major increase in the security guarantees of the Americans and the Israelis, which has helped initiate discussions and actions towards cooperation. The US has sought to calm frustration and risk from the two states by saying that its strong political relations and military support will help them gain better and safer conditions, promoting strategic relations between the nations.

Furthermore, the American Saudi-Israeli harmonic collaboration is unique. The US's global influence provides dominant support to bolster the coalition. US industrial, political, and socio-cultural powers foster business and confidence-boosting, thereby easing fears from both sides and increasing the chance for normalisation and collaboration.

Moreover, the US influence in fostering diplomatic relations reflects its skilful manoeuvring of geopolitical issues. The US manages to rally other important players in the Middle East to support Saudi-Israeli relations and is, therefore, able to create a favourable atmosphere of cooperation and mutual development.

The US will remain the most important country in fostering and sustaining diplomatic relations between Saudi Arabia and Is-

rael in the future. It remains the pivotal power with the strongest
diplomatic, economic, and military guarantees that can influence
the pace of normalised relations between the two primary powers
of the region. The US will continue to be at the centre of efforts
to sustain peace and support emerging legislation for new powers
in the Middle East while simultaneously encouraging these newly
established diplomatic links.

Potential Hurdles and Stalemates: Navigating Complexities

When attempting to achieve normalisation of relations between
Saudi Arabia and Israel, one can incur a multitude of possible
setbacks and complications that require special attention. The first
major barrier is the significant resentment towards Israel that exists
in some circles of Saudi society. While diplomatic relations may be
instituted, the lack of public opinion and social acceptance poses
a huge challenge. In addition, the Israeli-Palestinian conflict poses
a danger to the processes of normalisation. In the future, it will
likely be a serious problem in the relations between the sides.

Another major obstacle is the Middle East's more delicate and
multi-layered aspect: the combination of Saudi Arabia's geopolitical affiliations. The country's position as a regional superpower and its traditional frenemy relations make normalisation with
Israel much slower than desired due to a plethora of issues. The
added difficulties posed by the possible backlash from other states
hostile to Israel are all the more troublesome.

The different order of strategic priorities and security issues
confront the relations between Saudi Arabia and Israel as a far
greater obstacle. Despite the shared interest both states have in

limiting the range of Iran's influence in the region, the very different ways of achieving this make aligning the strategies require a great deal of care.

Negotiation and compromise are equally important for virtually all perspectives regarding a given regional conflict and the possible means of resolution.

Economic and trade relations also present challenges. Although there is an opportunity for economic cooperation and mutual gain, competition in the market, distribution of resources, and energy policies could break the normalisation process. These economic challenges require careful balancing to avoid friction points while ensuring alignment of interests.

Furthermore, the prospect of hostile regional opposition may create new barriers. Given the shifting geopolitical rivalries and interference, actions designed to disrupt the rapprochement between Saudi Arabia and Israel testify to the need for shrewd diplomacy and strategic counter-moves.

In other words, potential deadlocks and hurdles in all their intricacies will require sweeping diplomatic initiatives, masterful foresight, and marks of real engagement on both the Saudi and Israeli sides. The ability to overcome these hurdles and complexities will change the future towards enduring collaborative partnerships and normalisation.

Future Prospects: Analysing Long-term Trajectories

While contemplating the future growth of relations between Saudi Arabia and Israel, it is essential to evaluate their relations with ancillary powers like China and Russia; America is of great significance in this case. Further, these dynamic challenges, which include security threats alongside nations vying for regional dominance, greatly affect the extendable visions of their interrelations. Saudi Arabia and Israel need to come to terms with how to jointly counter interests while finding common ground on issues that support these changes. The transformations in such an intricate region as the Middle East during the last decade have forced all the countries to keep adapting constantly. Together with analysing the role that external players like the US, China, and Russia have on the growth of the relations between Saudi Arabia and Israel serves the second fundamental area that has been marked along with aiding the unipolar structure. It is also essential to monitor how these changes affect Saudi and Israel's dynamic relations.

All sociocultural relationships are influenced by, and in turn influence, the nature of diplomatic relations a country maintains in the international arena. Analysing shifting attitudes towards Saudi Arabia and Israel reveals some cultural steps that could be taken to improve understanding and mitigate conflict on both sides. Additionally, the strategies for business collaboration and commercial exchanges may be indicative of more profound multidisciplinary interactions in the future. Examining the nature of investment activities, performers' alliances, and overall business development processes would clarify the prospects of Saudi-Israeli economic cooperation. Moreover, relations between Israeli and Saudi Arabia may provide insight into other aspects that shall be used while studying relations between Israel and Saudi Arabia, especially Saudi Arabia's political alliance with Egypt. Observing how the axis states and regional coalitions respond to this new approach will assist in identifying some of the weaknesses in the Saudi-Israeli relationship. By studying these factors, one can analyse Saudi-Israeli relations and evaluate how favourable and beneficial they are to each other in the long run.

5

The Israeli-Palestinian Conflict

Policy Continuities and Shifts

Historical Context: Trump's Previous Approaches

During the first term of his presidency, Donald Trump made a seismic shift in the US approach to the Israeli-Palestinian conflict, a dilemma that had long defied resolution. His departure from traditional diplomacy and historical context was a bold move, offering a new vision for one of the world's most challenging geopolitical issues. Unlike his predecessors, Trump was unafraid to wade into the region with policies that fundamentally altered the approach, favouring aggressive posturing.

Perhaps the most controversial of his policies was the recognition of Jerusalem as Israel's capital in December 2017. This policy shift has single-handedly changed international relations between the US and many countries. Like many emerging democracies with a majority Muslim population, this was regarded as a hostile attack and a significant blow to the possibility of diplomatic solutions. It also complicated the already strained dynamics of the Israeli-Palestinian relationship and made negotiations for peace increasingly difficult.

Furthermore, the consequences of acknowledging Jerusalem as Israel's capital resulted in an increase in violence within the Palestinian territories. Mass protests fueled this in response to what they deemed a provocative announcement. Consequently, the move only enhanced the disenchantment and anger of the Palestinians, who viewed the US administration as further compounding their struggles for statehood and self-determination by suggestively siding with Israel. This episode demonstrated the volatility and the sensitivity of the issue of Jerusalem while reminding observers of the interplay between symbolic acts and actual on-the-ground dynamics of the conflict.

When Trump supported the idea of recognising Israel's claim over Jerusalem, he made it clear that he was frustrated with the current state of diplomatic relations as well as the stubbornness many showed toward conflicts. He did this hoping to jumpstart what he believed was a standstill in peace efforts. This decision showcased the administration's strong support for Israel and had ramifications for the entire region by shifting alliances and recalibrating power among the actors. Thus, Trump's proposed approach marked a new turning point for his successors regarding the Israeli-Palestinian conflict by redefining the terms of negotiations and the US's role in resolving the deep-rooted conflict.

Recognising Jerusalem and Its Aftermath

Throughout the United States' Israeli-Palestinian policy, President Trump's decision to recognise Jerusalem as Israel's capital in December 2017 stands out as one of the most controversial and pivotal moments. Similar to Trump's decision in 2017, there was a policy shift regarding the US's involvement in Jerusalem's peace process. The fallout from these moves led to both predicaments and dependencies across the entire Middle East region.

Trump's policies stirred global unease, sparking civil disobedience among Palestinians and leading to a reevaluation of diplomatic relations. The cancellation of aid for Palestinians, while politically beneficial for Trump within the Republican Party, was seen as a strain on established diplomatic relations. These actions set new precedents, often framed as a balancing approach, in the effort to diffuse the Israeli-Palestinian conflict.

In the initial period following the announcement, unrest broke out in multiple regions of the Middle East, particularly in the Palestinian territories, as a demonstration of anger and disappointment towards the US reversal. These protests showcased the level of sentiment attached to Jerusalem's issue and elucidated how difficult it is to deal with such an emotionally charged matter. At the same time, diplomatic engagements were activated to contain the damage and prevent further escalation of tensions, focusing on the fracture that required balance in dealing with the competing views regarding the city's status.

Recognising Jerusalem as Israel's capital further impacted the existing regional relations as it shifted geopolitical lines and recalibrated strategic reasoning among actors in the region. Some Arab states criticised the United States decision by reevaluating their relations with Washington in a more aggressive light, showing a real change in their diplomatic attitude and relations. At the same time, the decision bolstered the role of major regional players in the Israeli-Palestinian conflict by deepening the focus on mediating and shaping the dialogue, illustrating the multi-layered realities of the conflict from domestic, regional, and international perspectives.

The impacts of recognising Jerusalem as a capital were felt as much in political circles as they were culturally and sociologically, reflecting the deep vibrancy of the city. Jerusalem's tangible presence was synergised with modern geopolitics, and its symbolic significance was reshaped in a way that extended beyond the city limits when considered. As a result, the impact of this policy shift was felt far beyond the diplomacy designed to achieve it. It affected the multidimensional nature of the Palestinian–Israeli conflict and the rest of the Middle East region for years to come.

West Bank Annexation: Plans During the First Term

The debate surrounding the annexation of the West Bank surfaced for the first time as speculation during Donald Trump's first term. In January 2020, he presented his peace deal for the Middle East that included provisions for Israel to annex parts of the West Bank. This provoked a lot of internal and external discourse, attracting both support and further aggravating the already bitter discussion on the Israeli-Palestinian conflict.

The proposed annexation sent shockwaves through Palestinian communities and their fragile alliances. It was viewed as an aggressive action by Israel that disregarded international treaties and the possibility of a viable state for Palestinians. Opponents of the plan argued that it would undermine the potential for a two-state arrangement, a key goal for the region.

International responses to the suggested annexation were mixed. Some countries supported Israel's claim to certain areas, while others warned against actions that could be detrimental to stability in the region. The European Union, for example, warned of consequences if annexation proceeded without mutual agreement while simultaneously reiterating its commitment to a negotiated resolution.

Israel was also divided inside the country. Supporters of annexation highlighted security and historical factors, while opponents cited Israel's international standing and relations with neighbouring countries. This debate also had an impact on electoral politics, affecting coalition politics and public opinion toward the government's attitude toward territorial politics.

Claims made by Israel were intensified in the eyes of the Trump administration, who were clear about their conditional support for annexation. However, they encouraged communication between Palestinian and Israeli leaders while declaring that Israel has the freedom to make decisions autonomously. This strategy was part of the administration's broader approach to the region, which aimed to align with Israel's interests while maintaining diplomatic relationships with other regional partners, such as Saudi Arabia and the United Arab Emirates, both of which had expressed concerns about the annexation. Balancing these relationships presented complex challenges for the administration.

The pathway of the West Bank annexation plans during President Trump's first term highlights the distinct grievances, geopolitical calculations, and different imaginations of the future of the area. The possible consequences of such actions, including potential escalation of violence, further international isolation of Israel, and the erosion of the two-state solution, in the context of deeper regional and global power relationships warrant significant scrutiny in the swiftly changing geopolitical environment.

Policy Shifts Under a Second Administration

While trying to envisage the possible policy shifts under a second Trump presidency regarding the Israeli-Palestinian conflict, it is equally important to look at the emerging factors and key signs that will likely mark the boundaries of their planning horizon. One telling factor will centre around the 'Peace to Prosperity' plan and to what extent it will be maintained or adjusted to gain 'buy-in' from the constituents, stakeholders, and the region's realities. Furthermore, it is necessary to adjust the scope and focus of newly formed diplomatic partnerships. The degree of convergence with the Arab states and Israel along the primary and pivoting focus of Palestinian self-rule, sovereignty, security, and economic development is also important. In addition, how the internal political dynamics of Israel and those of the Palestinian territories impact the evolving multi-lateral dialogue deserves attention. While regionally dominating, what will the Trump administration's international engagement be in what it seeks to consider its legacy in the region? Some assessment of the willingness to engage and mediate suggestions will be needed.

In addition, the discussions about the legal status of Israeli settlements, land swap possibilities, and border definitions will likely impact the policy changes being considered. The lack of US fidelity to prior agreements and their approach to UN resolutions creates multifaceted complexities for achieving a viable and sustainable peace. We analyse here the discussions around the possible restructuring of aid allocation, which includes increased spending for humanitarian purposes and in the larger context of non-military assistance. Finally, an amalgamation of key foreign policy advisors, senior diplomats, and institutional actors will illuminate how these shifts or inertia will be understood. These factors reveal the challenges of discerning the policy intentions in the context of a hypothetical second Trump administration and how they might respond to the Israeli-Palestinian conflict.

A Two-State Solution: Feasibility Under Trump

The two-state solution has been a defining feature of global diplomacy regarding the Israel-Palestine conflict for decades. During the Trump presidency, however, the possibility of this solution encountered major difficulties and uncertainties. Unlike previous administrations, President Trump wholeheartedly embraced Israel and pursued policies that made the two-state solution impossible. They seemed to take every possible step to ensure that an independent Palestinian state was not an option throughout his presidency.

The Israeli capital's designation as Jerusalem, in particular, led to violence and conflict in the region. When President Trump moved the US embassy to Israel, it was seen as radical. This unorthodox decision further polarised America's political spectrum, resulting in international discourse where no middle ground existed. All attempts made to resolve the problem were disbanded. The decision undid any attempts made to fairly rationalise the ever-growing restrictions placed on Palestine and limited discussions regarding creating an East Jerusalem sovereign state where Palestinians could relocate and thrive.

Moreover, the close interaction of the Trump administration with Israeli leadership and the aid suspension to the Palestinian Authority complicated the two-state puzzle. The administration was aligned with Israeli Prime Minister Benjamin Netanyahu's One-Israel-First policies, where they advocated for unrestrained Israeli actions on the ground, which elicited criticism that this may inherently stifle negotiations altogether. Moreover, the weakening and redirection of financial assistance aimed at developing humanitarian aid for Palestinians raised questions about the intention to create a conducive atmosphere for a two-state solution.

Consequently, the strategic developments during the Trump presidency markedly reduced the possibility of the two-state solution existing in practicality. Unlike prior administrations, which unconditionally supported the creation of a Palestinian state, the policies advocated by the Trump administration cast doubt on whether any realistic plans existed for such an outcome. The impacts of these policy shifts were felt throughout the region, shaping the views of Israelis and Palestinians and modifying the environment for future peace initiatives. In light of these circumstances, the consideration and scrutiny surrounding whether a two-state solution could exist with Trump at the helm is, arguably, profoundly essential.

Security Concerns: Collaboration and Tensions

In diplomatic conversations and disagreements on wars, conflicts, and terrorism policy matters, security concerns seem to be imperative in framing the policy agenda about the Palestinian and Israeli conflict. The interplay of collaboration and tensions among the Israeli government, Palestinian leadership, and the United States controls the security framework of the region. Coordi-

nated efforts to improve security through intelligence cooperation and counter-terrorism activities have been crucial in dealing with prevalent challenges. Information exchange and joint
training programmes have often provided initial trust and confidence for cooperation. But behind all these collaborations lie
the significant sources of conflict: historical issues, land disputes,
and varying divergence in security concerns. Sustained cooperation is an overwhelming challenge due to the lingering violence,
deep-seated causes of distrust, and sustained hostility. The involvement of external players such as neighbouring countries and other
international organisations complicates the already complicated
security situation. Their actions can either reduce the conflict or
increase the extent of violence, alluding to the sensitive nature of
regional hegemony. Furthermore, in its stubbornness, the conflict
is multi-dimensional about the interplay of security issues and
socio-economic factors, humanitarian support, and politics.

Moreover, a technology change brings new challenges to security that must be addressed in a novel way. Tensions must be resolved
in a way that remains balanced politically, socially, economically,
and in terms of security. This neutral, interrelated approach is
important to ensure that the policies focus on reducing conflict
and fostering cooperation towards peace and stability, thus ending
regional tension in the long term.

Settlement Expansion: Domestic and Internation-
al Reactions

Settlement expansion in the Israeli-Palestinian conflict remains
controversial, inviting responses from both local and foreign actors. In Israel, the policy of settlement expansion has been met with

enthusiasm from the right-wing and settler movements which support the active expansion of Jewish population centres in the West Bank and East Jerusalem. They believe that such expansion is vital for Israel's strategic objectives and for exercising control over contentious regions.

On the other hand, within Israel's boundaries, there are left-wing political factions and human rights groups who, for one reason or another, oppose the expansion of settlements. Critics argue that continued construction and expansion of settlements impede prospects for a constructive two-state solution and worsen the situation with the Palestinian population. The ongoing public discourse on settlement expansion reveals a contradiction about how Israeli security and the possibility of a negotiated settlement would be conceptualised vis-à-vis the prolonged Israeli occupation.

The expansion of Israeli settlements has and continues to receive strong international political sentiment. The United Nations, European Union, and other nation-states have shown concern regarding the negative impact settlement expansion has had and will continue to have on the peace and stability of the region. Various international platforms have continuously called upon Israel to put an end to these activities, asserting that such actions are contrary to international law and serve as a barrier to establishing a peaceful resolution to this conflict.

In addition, the US policy on settlement expansions has shifted in terms of how various administrations have aligned with Israeli policies. While prior US administrations have criticised and sought to limit expansion because it would hinder peace negotiations, the approach taken by Trump marked a significant shift. Recognising Israeli control over certain settlements in the West Bank, alongside not strongly condemning this policy, represented a shift in

US policy, drawing mixed reactions from the global community and further complicating the gridlock surrounding the diplomatic efforts aimed at resolving the enduring conflict.

The expansion of settlements is still one of the focal issues of the Israeli-Palestinian conflict, defining the scope of the negotiations, exacerbating violence, and shaping the balance of power perceptions in the region. The intricacies that underpin this issue highlight not only the intractability of the conflict but also the difficulties of achieving a fair and sustainable solution.

Settlement Expansion: Domestic and International Reactions

The Israeli-Palestinian conflict has always been humanitarian, and the US has been particularly sensitive to helping the people involved in this rather disheartening scenario. The US has always been determined when it comes to aid programmes for the Palestinians and has strived hard to fulfil the needs of the Palestinian citizens through aid in the provision of health facilities, educational institutions, infrastructure building, etc. This trend experienced a break in the Trump era.

During the first term, the administration placed severe restrictions on the spending of aid to the Palestinians because of perceived misappropriation of funds and suspected organisational accountability. This led to rampant criticism since many people believed that the well-being of the people of Palestine was already in a precarious state and lacked the means to survive financially; this decision would destroy any remaining hope for stability in the region.

At the same time, restrictions on how aid could be given, such as cutting off aid to certain Palestinian bodies, also altered the complex humanitarian scenario and instead shifted the funds towards sponsoring US-tailored policies. These actions began a debate on the use of aid and its moral stance but also caused diplomatic disputes for the international parties concerned with the region.

During these events, other global players came into the picture to try to plug the gaps caused by the US aid withdrawal 'for the better'—or 'for the worse', depending on the point of view—and protect damaged vulnerable populations. Regardless, the changed environment around aid provision amends the existing power dynamics within the humanitarian system, considering additional coordination challenges for providing ongoing assistance and essential services.

With the consideration of the potential for a second term, the debate concerning the US aid for the Israelis and Palestinians is bound to return. It becomes fundamental to study the ramifications of some sort of continuity or changes in aid regarding the developed humanitarian landscape and the overall peace process. Hence, scrutinising the Israeli–Palestinian conflict requires careful observation of the persisting shifts in regional politics with the complex system of aid politics.

Diplomatic Engagements: Allies and Regional Players

The Israeli-Palestinian conflict continues to be a focal point worldwide, attracting the interest of many international relations diplomats. This conflict, in conjunction with negotiations with pertinent allies or regional players, remains necessary for the future developments of the rest of the region. The ongoing diplomatic engagements provide a glimmer of hope for potential peace and stability in the region.

Along with the rest of the world working on peace initiatives, as it often happens in all international conflicts, the United States, the European Union, and Arab states, in one way or the other, have been influential in the international peace negotiations and initiatives. Their active involvement reassures the audience of the international community's commitment to resolving the conflict.

It is imperative to mediate dialogue and fuel regional stability to address the urgent need for peace in the region. The audience should feel the urgency of the situation and the need for immediate action.

The US has always been and probably will be a significant aspect of concern for Israeli-Palestinian affairs. Sullivan tries to calm down all parties in conflict. Historically, it offers alternatives to fight or fork other ways. Before trying to talk first to the less influential party between the two to see if any alternative solutions can be found. Less antagonistic if it has a deal with Israel, which has focused recently.

Persuade Dialogue Operator: The previous administration focused almost entirely on Israel and disregarded any inclination for Palestinian engagement. One could call this a Motivational Politics Approach. After the period of attempting to integrate borders, the previously stated policy ordered unconditional deals to engage with Israel and overlooked Palestine, touting positive outcomes for peace as a result.

The landscape could possibly be changed after a change of administration. The opposing Biden-Harris will certainly take chances, encouraging support incentives for the US's traditional allies to reconsider multilateral engagements through restructuring or re-initiating encounter routines with partners.

Jordan and Egypt's bordering role in peace agreements has been instrumental in the geopolitical conflict. Due to their amities with Israel, the nation-states have made a number of diplomatic attempts and initiated relevant steps towards maintaining peace in the region. These countries are bound to participate in and assist in constructive mediation between the belligerents based on their existing treaties of peace with Israel.

Moreover, agreements of moderation such as 'The Abram Accords' have provided innovative avenues for cooperation not only among Arab states but for Israel, paving the way to stronger relations. The newly formed friendships and the warming relations between Israel and the United Arab Emirates, Bahrain, and Sudan suggest a new geopolitical paradigm afoot – one that is very positive but, at the same time, will have great consequences for the Israeli-Palestinian conflict. Economic partnerships alongside shared security will transform unprecedented enemy collaboration into ally collaboration.

We cannot overlook the European Union and other world organisations' role in providing humanitarian assistance, supporting diplomacy and socially meaningful activities. The involvement of the EU simultaneously motivates dialogue and assists with constructive initiatives, highlighting the essence of multilateral cooperation in the intricacies of the Israeli-Palestinian conflict. Considering the impact of these global diplomatic efforts, enduring peace and conflict resolution remains the ultimate goal, which will always require continuous multilateral approaches, revised bilateral relations, and thoughtful shifts in the surrounding context of the region.

Conclusion: Continuities, Changes, and Future Outlooks

It has been many decades, one would argue, centuries, that the Is-raeli-Palestinian conflict has persisted without finding a resolution to its struggles. Since this context has been accompanied by wars and infrequent peace treaties as Israel and Palestine have endured throughout the years, this conflict has remained omnipresent. Fo-cusing on this chapter, we have scrutinised the lasting tactics and the shifts that took place while dealing with the conflict, includ-ing all diplomatic relations with allies and regional players. An enduring problem that had captured component nations includ-ed a dominance struggle. The Israeli versus Palestinian statehood struggle is one of the many challenges that Israel itself has fought. Further negotiations still stubbornly fail to vanish due to funda-mental issues such as the whereabouts of Jerusalem.

Furthermore, the inflow and outflow of neighbouring territo-ries such as the Jordan region and Saudi Arabia further add to the angular complexities surrounding this conflict. On the other hand, changes around the Middle East—including the Jordanian normalisation treaty with other Arab countries—are capable of improving or worsening Israel's approach to Palestine. Peace co-existence would undoubtedly require rethinking innovative tech-niques to give Palestinian citizens the freedom to develop their state. But for now, reconsidered diplomacy from all delegated peo-ple is essential.

The efforts needed to build trust and dialogue while taking care of the well-being of both Israelis and Palestinians will be challeng-ing. Meeting humanitarian needs and developing the economy in

Palestinian territories is equally vital in achieving peace in Israel and Palestine. When looking at pieces of the conflict in Israel and Palestine, there is more to address – the role of Iran and Turkey and how they serve as external influences. A more practical approach to a solution requires a more prolonged investment of time, careful creativity in diplomacy, and a better sense of judgement guided by history, culture, and politics. With these hurdles ahead, coming up with a formulated strategy still serves the purpose - achieving peace comes with numerous advantages. To resolve the Israeli-Palestinian dispute, global leaders need to think critically while finding practical approaches to deeply-rooted struggles and actively work towards establishing lasting peace.

6

Iran Strategy
Revisiting Maximum Pressure

Historical Context: Maximum Pressure Under Trump

The 'maximum pressure' strategy regarding Iran was one of the prominent aspects of Trump's foreign policy approaches, which differed significantly from the previous administration's policy in this region. This policy was implemented in 2018 with the hope of coercing Iran to reform the Joint Comprehensive Plan of Action (JCPOA) or at least amend what the United States government regarded as deal-breaking aspects of the agreement. The 'maximum pressure' strategy aimed at systematically dismantling the Iranian government's economic, diplomatic, and military capabilities by forcefully undermining its main policies to stop funding militant groups, missile programmes, and alter its general stance on Middle East policies. This policy construct was based on the assumption that unrelenting sanctions combined with growing international ostracism would bring Tehran to the negotiating table. The policy was executed through a combination of approaches that involved restoring extensive sanctions on Iran's economically vital sectors; energy, finance, and shipping, along with international trade. Furthermore, Trump's administration attempted to galvanise support from other states to economically strangle Iran by withdrawing from the JCPOA and encouraging other signatories to do the same.

The increase in militarisation of the region, alongside elevated rhetoric and propaganda, heightened tension in the area and exacerbated the fear of conflict. The administration was determined to continue the strategy despite strong dissent from long-time allies and global institutions. The maximum pressure development during Trump's first term showcased complex systems of domestic politics, realigned global powers, and Iran's counter-responses. As a result, there was a fierce debate over the effectiveness of the policy, where advocates claimed it curtailed Iranian activity in the region. At the same time, opponents pointed to the harsh humanitarian impact of the policy and the failure to achieve its goals.

Comprehensive Sanctions: Objectives and Implementation

The execution of absolute sanctions on Iran has been a key feature of the maximum pressure approach, aiming to achieve a number of strategic goals. These sanctions are designed to restrict Iran's nuclear and ballistic missile capabilities, which are seen as existential risks to global and local order. The strategy is to apply economic strain on the regime by freezing the country's energy, finance, and shipping industries, with the hope that this will force

Iran to reconsider its actions in a way that promotes global peace. Apart from changing Iran's strategic thinking, the sanctions also aim to reduce the regime's funding capacity for proxies and other non-state actors in the region. The objective is to cut off funding and disrupt illicit funding routes to reduce Iran's influence in destabilising other countries and waging wars in the region. These also seek to increase Iran's price for aggressive moves, thus deterring further attempts at regional dominance and expansion.

The all-encompassing approach taken by the sanctions includes the cooperation of various international partners, emphasising trade, investment, and technology barriers with Iran. This constructs a cohesive opposition against Iran's undertakings, showcasing the international unity regarding contending Iran's actions. The enforcement of the sanctions by a coalition of countries strengthens the impact of these actions and helps to convey the importance of respecting global standards of conduct.

Comprehensive sanctions pose problematic issues and implications despite having a sound, logical basis. Red flags around the possible humanitarian consequences of the sanctions on the people of Iran require examination so as not to place an undue and disproportionate burden on innocent civilians. In addition, there is a need to factor in how the imposition of sanctions will be executed, as the success of sanctions is determined by the level of implementation and effectiveness of avoidance measures taken by the entities. These approaches to fighting evasion and ensuring cooperation with the sanctions policies are integral to policy implementation.

As the world navigates the complex issues related to the imposition of all-encompassing sanctions, it is crucial to constantly assess their effectiveness and modify them according to emerging conditions. Striking a balance between forceful pressure, diplomatic dialogue, and exploring steps toward reducing tension will greatly impact the effectiveness of these sanctions in changing Iran's actions and establishing peace in the Middle East. This ongoing assessment and modification process ensures that the policy remains adaptive and effective.

Diplomatic Isolation: Strengthening Allies and Isolating Iran

While attempting to limit Iran's activities, "diplomatic isolation" has been one of their main tools in attempting to contain its volatile activities in the Middle East. The United States, with the support of its allies and partners within the region, has tried to form a cohesive counter-alliance to Iranian expansion and hold the regime responsible for its actions. This approach strives to counter Iran's diplomacy while simultaneously forging new regional partnerships. The efforts made with regard to Iran have centred on gathering international support, which aims at containing Iran's aggressive posturing and the threats it poses to the stability of the Middle East. The coordination of international diplomacy to bring the attention of the world to the phenomena of Iran and its terrorist policies, which create and sustain violence in the world, is pivotal to this initiative. The main goal is to engage relevant powers to emphasise the need for the alliance to take common steps against Iran's aggressive actions of ignoring international laws and unilateral actions. Additionally, strengthening collaboration at a multilateral level has been essential in exposing the existence of a consensus on the issues of Iran's ballistic missiles, terrorism, and her meddling in other nation's sovereignty.

Focusing on diplomatic isolation reinforces the idea that the entire world is united in ensuring Iran is punished for its mischief. Concurrently, concerted attempts have been made to improve diplomacy with countries near Iran to isolate Iran further and reduce its influence. The idea is to strengthen ties with countries that are also apprehensive about Iran's behaviour to carve out a coalition of like-minded states dedicated to maintaining peace and order in the Middle East. Employing shared security interests and common strategic goals to muster a unified front against Tehran's hostile agenda embodies this approach. Diplomacy also seeks to exacerbate the socio-economic costs of siding with Iran, thus persuading governments to adjust their policies and lean towards the international community. Strangling Iran with diplomatic isolation is complemented by constant engagement with regional actors and international organisations, stressing the need for a united response against Iran's reckless actions. The plan seeks to use diplomacy to create a strong coalition that will increase the impact of Iran's actions while strengthening allies and isolating Tehran diplomatically.

Impact on the Iranian Economy: Analyzing Economic Consequences

The US maximum pressure strategy on Iran aimed at completely disrupting the country's economy. The United States placed harsh restrictions on Iran's key industries, such as oil exports, banking, and shipping. These sanctions had intense repercussions on the Iranian economy.

The most serious damage caused to the Iranian economy was the decrease in revenue from oil, which was one of Iran's main sources of income. Due to the increased sanctions, oil exports were limited to the point where foreign exchange revenue was impossible to generate, increasing budget deficits, inflationary devaluation of the currency, and devaluation of the local currency, which is critical for the national economy and public welfare. In addition, financial sanctions greatly restricted Iran's access to the global banking infrastructure, which made international and inter-country trade transactions impossible.

Moreover, the negative effects of the sanctions were easily observed in many businesses and industries within Iran. Reduced access to vital imports and technology and improved supply chains stunted economic growth and caused high unemployment. Such issues not only hurt the day-to-day lives of Iranians but also increased anti-government frustration, leading to further civil unrest.

In light of the economic pressures stemming from the 'maximum pressure policy,' the Iranian government initiated domestic strategies to soften the impact. These included attempts to bolster non-oil exports, currency devaluation, and austerity measures. However, these strategies further strained the economy and inflation, decreased purchasing power and living standards, and worsened and prolonged preexisting inflationary challenges.

Furthermore, the economic recession impacted other countries globally and economically. Iran's immediate trading partners saw serious disruption in economic relations with their trading partners and allies, and the rest of the world became increasingly concerned as they faced volatility in supply and uncertainty stemming from the geopolitical landscape. These changes also caused countries in the Middle East to revise their approaches to trade and investment due to the changing sanctions context and expectations of stability within the region.

Economic repercussions, international influence, and scrutiny graphed the validity of the maximum pressure strategy. Observers analysed the approach and attempted to comprehend its consequences and effectiveness. Studying the impact on the Iranian economy and analysing current socio-economic factors and political systems, alongside regional integrations, is crucial. This examination will aid in understanding the vast consequences of the sudden enforcement of maximum-pressure policies on Iran's economy.

Regional Responses: Reactions from Middle Eastern States

In contrast to other nations, the response given by Middle Eastern nations came in different frameworks. Countries like the United Arab Emirates and Saudi Arabia showcased excitement mixed with caution, revealing a desire to limit Iran's regional power. The maximum pressure approach had an effect as these countries shifted their policies to be more aligned with the United States, which directly opposes Iran.

On the opposing side, Qatar and Oman have taken a softer approach, citing concerns over the U.S.-Iran conflict's potential destabilising risks. These nations have walked a tightrope of diplomatic relations, shuttled between conflicting parties in attempts to foster compromise and preserve order in the region.

In addition, Israel's reaction to the maximum pressure campaign has been complex and multifaceted. Although Israel tends to support the more aggressive approach to Iran, harsher policies raise the risk of significant backlash, whether through retaliation by Iran or its proxies. Shifting dynamics afford Israel many strategic opportunities, but with the need to adjust its defence policies and other allied resources, Israel must rethink its collaborative efforts with other important regional allies.

Like the other Gulf states, Turkey's policy towards the maximum pressure campaign adds to the complexity of Turkey's position due to its overarching goal of Gulf Cooperation Council states. It has a historical rivalry with some Gulf nations. Ankara has been noted for opposing the idea of an aggressive approach towards Iran and has attempted to pursue its strategies for maintaining regional order while protecting Turkey's interests.

The regional responses to the maximum pressure campaign showcase the balance of alliances, rivalries, and competing security issues within the Middle East. While the region responds to these oil price shifts, decision-makers must strategically balance the divergent viewpoints to build agreement and mitigate conflict. Ultimately, the greater the region's response, the more repercussions the maximum pressure strategy will entail, complicating the already existing strategy for soft power, intricate Iraq diplomacy, and pragmatic bargaining with Iran.

Military Deterrence: Evaluating Security Postures and Strategies

Considering how Iran's influence continues to evolve, the question of military deterrence is equally important for regional actors and superpowers. The evaluation of security postures and strategies must consider the multifaceted alliances, rivalries, and historic animosities that form the region's security architecture. In the case of Gulf states, the existence of an Iranian threat has catalysed a significant degree of military modernisation and the formation of strategic alliances with other world powers, including the United States. The longstanding fears of Iran's support for militant proxies and its nuclear capabilities have also led Israel to make substantial investments in defence and proactive security measures.

The approach of a conflict in which power can rely on asymmetric warfare can best be described as long-drawn-out. The deterrence strategy is a powerful state's challenge to proxy and unconventional forces. Thus, almost all regional military policies combine elements of counterinsurgency with cyber defence systems and shields against missiles to cover the gaps left by traditional military strategy.

Furthermore, the profoundly interconnected character of regional conflicts highlights the need for a comprehensive understanding of military deterrence and integrated strategy. The Yemeni, Syrian, and Iraqi conflicts pose complex intersecurity dilemmas requiring comprehensive calculations of local, regional, and international interactions and interdependencies. Such interconnections also require, for example, rapid response by allied forces, active information sharing, and coordination to guarantee an adequate response to destabilising activity.

In the context of rivalry among the most powerful nations, the merger of military, economic, and diplomatic activities further challenges the formulation of effective deterrence policies. For the US as one of the global players, the strategic calculus entails balancing attention given to regional allies alongside the need to control escalation and pursue other overarching geopolitical interests. At the same time, the increasing Russian and Chinese roles in the Middle East region add further complexity to the regional security dynamics, which requires scrutiny regarding existing deterrence policies.

Ultimately, assessing security frameworks and Iran's activities in the region requires an all-encompassing perspective due to the complexities of conflict evolution. Effective military deterrence, in particular, requires the continuous monitoring of emerging threats, careful balancing of interconnected regional crises, and active collaboration with partners to stabilise the Middle East.

The Nuclear Question: Containment Versus Negotiation

Iran's nuclear issue has been persistent in analyses of global politics for quite some time. The discourse on Iran's contentious nuclear activities centres on two possible approaches: containment and negotiation. Some politically motivated analysts prefer the idea of containment, which suggests constraining Iran's nuclear propulsion through severe sanctions, military force, and diplomatic isolation. Sometimes defined as the prevention of enabling frameworks, proponents argue that containment is critical to halting weaponisation and maintaining regional balance. Negotiations, however, involve some form of talking or diplomacy with the Iranian regime towards an agreement restricting their fuel processing to non-weaponisable levels while permitting energy development. This solution attempts to resolve a concern by defusing the threat of a nuclear race in the region. The application of certain measures, such as economic sanctions and authoritative military presence, has had mixed success in curtailing Iran's nuclear undertakings. There is general agreement that international efforts have, to some extent, slowed down Iran's plans to develop nuclear weapon capabilities. Still, most acknowledge there is a greater risk of escalated military conflict. Furthermore, the Iranian people face extreme ethical dilemmas due to the severe containment measures that have been placed.

On the other hand, previous negotiation efforts, such as the Joint Comprehensive Plan of Action (JCPOA), sought to resolve the nuclear impasse using multilateral diplomacy alongside Iran's nuclear capability restrictions with diplomatically acceptable scope limitations. Nevertheless, the debate around the success of the JCPOA and its enduring value has remained deeply divisive and adds to contrasting perceptions surrounding the possibility of diplomatic negotiations. As the world deals with the nuclear conundrum, it must contend with the dual complexities of containment and negotiation measures. This requires a deep appreciation of the internal factors driving Iran's politics, regional ambitions, and security needs. In addition, every policy formulation attempt should thoroughly consider the risks and opportunities presented by each available course of action for policymakers. Ultimately, resolving the nuclear conundrum depends on the convergence of competing interests, the reduction of strategic mistrust, and authentic diplomacy. The dynamics of containment and negotiation are at the core of one of the world's most critical global security and stability challenges, highlighting the need for better-coordinated policy responses and joint action at the international level.

Human Rights and Domestic Unrest: Internal Dynamics in Iran

For some time, Iran has received much critique on human rights and domestic dissent. The internal dynamics of a nation are multifaceted, and different aspects within the nation, such as political, social, and cultural spheres, are crucial for Iran's internal stability and international image. An expectation for reforms and respect for human rights has characterised the Iranian people. Different groups within society grew frustrated with the unjust actions being taken against individuals. The government's handling of domestic unrest, especially after the 2009 presidential elections and subsequent protests, made it clear that the regime was willing to assert its authority. It showed how poorly the government dealt with civil society, wanting more freedoms and less control over their lives. This part addresses the deep multidimensional facets of the internal issues in Iran and contemporary forms of dissent. It discusses the government's responses to dissent and the socio-political realities of activism and advocacy for change from below.

In addition, evaluating the effects of social class, population changes, and age-related differences is vital for understanding the socio-political changes in Iran. The international community has closely monitored human rights issues and internal unrest as they have become prominent topics in international relations and geopolitical discussions. The blend of human rights issues and foreign policy has become a contested debate that has altered how many states and international organisations treat Iran individually and through coalitions. Understanding the intertwined aspects of human rights coupled with internal unrest in Iran is essential in unravelling the consequences for regional peace, international relations, and moral responsibility. In the end, analysing these phenomena from within Iran's borders is crucial for understanding the complexity of Iran's socio-political system and its relations with other Middle Eastern countries.

Evaluations and Criticisms: International and Domestic Perspectives

The 'maximum pressure' approach regarding Iran has received mixed evaluations and criticisms both internationally and domestically. Looking at the outside world, the stance taken by the United States has elicited a mixed bag of opinions and analyses. Some nations have voiced support for dealing with Iran's regional aspirations and nuclear programmes. In contrast, other nations worry about the effectiveness of such harsh steps, especially regarding diplomatic relations. Some key allies, most notably the European powers, have also been torn in their loyalty to the strategy, exposing different ideas about how best to deal with Iran. All these differing opinions have illustrated the difficulties of shaping a unified international agreement to deal with Iran's conduct. In addition, multilateral institutions have engaged with the maximum pressure strategy, subjecting it to criticism, as debates in the United Nations and other bodies have displayed opposing views. On the domestic front, the strategy has also encountered a mixed reception. Here in the United States, some stakeholders have underscored the value of the strategy as a means of restraining Iranian aggression and advancing US interests in the region. At the same time, however, some other critics have lambasted the increasing humanitarian costs of the strategy and the strain it imposes on traditional allies.

Furthermore, the debate among the political elites has revealed new differences regarding how to interact with Iran, suggesting further disagreement on how to resolve the issue optimally. In the same way, the conflict about the strategy started vigorous disputes and discussions across the academia and policy world, leading to an intense exchange of ideas and perspectives. A diverse range of scholars and experts contributed to the discourse by providing an intricate understanding of the geopolitical, economic, and security dimensions accompanying the maximum pressure approach. They also tackled the public perceptions, which, in their many forms, called into the debate over the strategy and its recalibration or resolute pursuit. The vast array of interpretations, analyses, and critiques emphasises the difficulties in formulating foreign policy directives, highlighting the clash of interests and ideologies that are features of international relations. Sifting through this is necessary to find the proper mix of military aims, diplomacy, and stability on a global level.

Path Forward: Exploring Potential Adjustments to Strategy

When considering ways to adjust the strategy for Iran that the US plans to pursue in the future, we assess that some elements are effective and that balancing their utility with possible negative fall-out consequences is crucial. Determining the effectiveness of the current strategy requires addressing the multi-faceted component of deal-making and pressure. One example of this consideration is assessing the balance between engagement and pressure. A purely coercive approach fails to provide opportunities for constructive engagement. On the other hand, focus should also be directed to the possibility of easing tensions and fostering regional peace.

Moreover, focusing on the humanitarian impact of the sanctions on the Iranian population and how to maintain pressure without causing undue damage to the humanitarian side of things is critically important. This means that circular sanctions that seek to control the ruling regime and not the people should be properly crafted. At the same time, initiating dialogues and empowering Iranian citizens through cultural, academic, and civil society institutions helps cultivate positive feelings and helps spread the common good.

At the same time, the United States must continue to pursue a wider focus on developing an effective international consensus and cooperation framework to deal with Iran's behaviour. This involves renewing diplomatic avenues and forming pacts with relevant stakeholders to confront regional security and human rights issues collectively. The US can work with allies and partners to execute its strategy effectively because it allows them to unify their efforts and present a cohesive message to promote adherence to international norms.

Besides, concerning the Iranian nuclear programme, their policies remain critically relevant and require a strategic reevaluation approach. A balanced approach combining strict monitoring, sanctions relief contingent on verifiable compliance, and active negotiation retains non-proliferation objectives while incentivising Iran to fulfil its responsibilities.

Addressing the issue requires an in-depth analysis of Iran's internal factors and evolving socio-political realities. This entails a more robust investment in information collection and specialised knowledge of the Iranian population, allowing policymakers to respond to the needs and discontent of the country's citizens.

By incorporating all these aspects and moving forward with a new approach that involves diplomatic flexibility, selective pressure, multilateral cooperation, and deep understanding, the US could cultivate stability, advance its agenda, and improve prospects for a more positive relationship with Iran.

7

Energy Dominance

Impact on Gulf States and Global Markets

Historical Context: Trump's Energy Policy Legacy

During Donald Trump's first term as President of the United States, his administration pursued a robust and ambitious energy policy to achieve energy independence and dominance. The Trump administration focused on unleashing domestic energy production by rolling back regulations, promoting fossil fuel development, and supporting the expansion of the shale oil and gas industry. One of the central components of Trump's energy policy legacy was the emphasis on deregulation. The administration sought to remove barriers to energy extraction and production, often framing regulatory rollbacks to stimulate economic growth and job creation. This approach resulted in significant shifts in environmental protections and land use policies, impacting areas such as offshore drilling, methane emissions, and coal mining. Trump's administration also prioritized expanding infrastructure for energy transport and export. Efforts to streamline permitting processes for pipelines and liquefied natural gas (LNG) terminals aimed to bolster the US's position as a major energy exporter. The push for infrastructure expansion reflected a broader strategy to bolster energy security and promote American energy interests on the global stage.

Furthermore, the Trump administration pursued a policy of reevaluating international agreements and commitments related to energy and climate change. This included withdrawing from the Paris Climate Agreement and challenging multilateral agreements that imposed carbon emissions and fossil fuel usage restrictions. By distancing the US from global accords and frameworks, the administration sought to prioritize American energy sovereignty and diminish perceived constraints on domestic energy development. The aggressive pursuit of energy dominance under the Trump administration drew both support and criticism. Proponents lauded the focus on energy independence and the boost to the domestic energy sector, emphasizing the potential for increased national security and economic benefits.

On the other hand, critics raised concerns about the environmental impact, citing potential harm to ecosystems, public health, and exacerbation of climate change. As the tenure of Trump's presidency unfolded, the administration's energy policies significantly shaped the landscape of domestic and global energy markets. The lasting legacy of Trump's energy agenda will continue to reverberate in subsequent administrations and influence ongoing debates surrounding energy policy, sustainability, and environmental stewardship.

Strategic Imperatives: The Quest for Energy Independence

As the United States strives to strengthen its position as a global energy leader, the quest for energy independence has emerged as a strategic imperative. Energy independence, in this context, refers to the ability of a country to meet its energy needs from domestic sources, reducing reliance on foreign oil and enhancing national security through energy self-sufficiency. This drive for energy independence has far-reaching implications for both domestic policy and international dynamics. At the core of this quest is the belief that reducing dependence on oil imports can insulate the US from geopolitical vulnerabilities and economic disruptions stemming from global oil price fluctuations and supply disruptions. Achieving energy independence involves a multi-faceted approach encompassing technological innovation, regulatory reforms, and investment in infrastructure. The expansion of domestic oil and gas production and advancements in renewable energy sources are pivotal components of this strategy. Moreover, efforts to streamline permitting processes and promote energy efficiency further contribute to the pursuit of self-reliance. Energy independence also holds significance in fortifying the nation's resilience in the face of adversarial actions by oil-exporting nations or geopolitical adversaries. The US seeks to mitigate potential risks associated with supply disruptions and geopolitical tensions by diversifying energy sources and decreasing reliance on specific oil-rich regions.

Moreover, an emphasis on energy independence aligns with broader economic and industrial objectives, fostering job creation, economic growth, and technological innovation within the energy sector. Furthermore, it provides the foundation for environmental stewardship by promoting cleaner energy alternatives and reducing carbon emissions, which are harmful gases released into the atmosphere, contributing to climate change. The quest for energy independence necessitates a careful balance between promoting domestic energy production and addressing environmental concerns. This balance requires thoughtful policymaking and collaboration across public and private sectors to ensure sustainable and responsible development. As the US continues to chart a course towards energy independence, it must navigate complex geopolitical, economic, and environmental considerations. Pursuing self-sufficiency in energy resources represents a defining challenge and opportunity, shaping the nation's role in global energy markets and influencing its relationships with key energy-producing regions worldwide.

Geopolitical Ramifications for the Gulf States

The pursuit of energy dominance by the Trump administration has had profound geopolitical ramifications for the Gulf States, a term used to collectively refer to the countries bordering the Persian Gulf, whose economies are intricately tied to the global oil market. These ramifications encompass a complex web of relationships, conflicts, and opportunities, shaping regional dynamics in ways that reverberate across the international stage. First and foremost, the policy shift towards energy independence in the United States has altered the traditional power balance in the Gulf region. Historically, the reliance of the US on Gulf oil reserves has been a cornerstone of its engagement with Gulf countries, underpinning security guarantees and strategic partnerships. However, as the US reduces its dependency on Gulf oil, the calculus of its commitment to the region undergoes a recalibration, prompting Gulf States to reassess their strategic posture and alliances. Moreover, the evolving energy landscape has injected new complexities into the delicate power balance among the Gulf States. The rise of the US as a major energy producer has diminished the leverage of traditional oil-exporting nations, thereby reshaping competition and collaboration within the Gulf Cooperation Council (GCC) and fueling shifts in intra-regional dynamics. As Gulf States navigate these shifts, they must grapple with the challenges of diversifying their economies and adapting to the changing geopolitical circumstances.

Furthermore, energy dominance has also intensified the rivalry between Saudi Arabia and Iran, both vying for influence and market share amidst shifting global dynamics. The economic pressures from the fluctuating oil market have exacerbated existing political fault lines, amplifying the stakes in regional proxy conflicts and exacerbating tensions. The interplay of energy politics, security considerations, and historical enmities underscores the intricate entanglement of energy geopolitics in the Gulf. Moreover, the emergence of renewable energy technologies and the global push for sustainability present challenges and opportunities for the Gulf States. As the world transitions towards cleaner energy sources, Gulf economies built on hydrocarbon exports confront the imperative of diversification and innovation. This transition necessitates rethinking economic models, investment strategies, and international positioning, compelling Gulf States to adapt to the evolving energy landscape while capitalizing on their comparative advantages. In conclusion, the pursuit of energy dominance by the US has ushered in a new era of geopolitical complexity for the Gulf States, impacting their relationships, security dynamics, and economic prospects. Navigating these geopolitical ramifications requires astute diplomacy, strategic foresight, and proactive adaptation to an ever-changing global energy order.

Economic Impacts on Global Oil Markets

The economic impacts of the United States energy dominance policy on global oil markets have been profound and far-reaching. The shift in the US energy landscape, characterized by the rise of shale oil production and the re-emergence of the US as a major oil exporter, has significantly altered the dynamics of global energy trade and pricing. One of the most noticeable effects has been the dilution of OPEC's traditional monopoly over the oil market. The surge in US shale oil production has increased competition for traditional oil-exporting countries, compelling them to reassess their market strategies and pricing mechanisms. Additionally, the influx of US shale oil onto the international market has contributed to fluctuations in oil prices, challenging the stability that oil-dependent economies traditionally sought. Beyond the supply-side dynamics, the US energy renaissance has also impacted the demand side of the equation. As the US steadily reduces its reliance on imported oil, global demand patterns are undergoing significant shifts, leading to adjustments in consumer and producer behaviours. Moreover, the increased energy self-sufficiency of the US has reshaped the geopolitical calculus of oil-producing nations across the globe. Traditional alliances and dependencies are being reevaluated as the impact of America's energy independence reverberates through established energy corridors.

Furthermore, the diversification of export destinations for American oil has introduced new elements of competition and cooperation among global actors in the energy sphere. In response to these structural changes, oil-exporting countries must adopt more diversified and resilient economic policies to mitigate the vulnerabilities stemming from their dependence on oil revenues. This trend has also laid the foundation for strategic collaborations between energy producers and consumers, fostering alternative arrangements for energy security in an evolving global landscape. Ultimately, the economic impacts of the US energy dominance extend beyond mere market dynamics; they encompass pivotal geopolitical and diplomatic implications that continue to shape the behaviour and strategies of traditional and emerging players in the global oil market.

The Shale Revolution: Reshaping US-Gulf Relations

The shale revolution, marked by the rapid expansion of unconventional oil and gas production in the United States, has significantly altered the dynamics of global energy markets, particularly in traditional oil-producing regions such as the Gulf states. The surge in domestic shale production has positioned the US as a formidable competitor in the global energy landscape, challenging the historical dominance of Gulf countries in oil exports. This transformation has reshaped economic realities and spurred recalibrations in geopolitical relationships between the US and the Gulf Cooperation Council (GCC) member states. The impact of the shale revolution on US-Gulf relations is multifaceted. On the one hand, the surge in US shale production has contributed to shifting the balance of power in the global energy market, enabling the US to reduce its reliance on Gulf oil imports. This newfound energy independence has provided the US with greater leverage in its diplomatic engagements with Gulf nations, allowing for a reevaluation of bilateral security and economic cooperation. Concurrently, diversifying global oil supply sources through shale production has enhanced energy security for importing countries, thereby reducing uncertainties associated with geopolitical instability in the Gulf region. However, the emergence of the US as a major energy player has also introduced complexities in its relations with traditional Gulf allies. While the US remains committed to supporting the security architecture of the Gulf, the changing energy dynamics have prompted Gulf states to reassess their own economic strategies and regional partnerships.

Furthermore, the competitive pressures from increased US shale output have required Gulf producers to adapt to evolving market conditions, driving reforms to enhance cost efficiency, diversify revenue streams, and invest in downstream industries. Moreover, the shale revolution has influenced the broader strategic calculus of the US and the Gulf states, leading to collaborative initiatives in technological innovation, energy infrastructure development, and renewable energy investments. These joint endeavours seek to capitalize on the complementary strengths of the US's shale expertise and the Gulf's long-standing experience in conventional oil production, thereby fostering mutually beneficial synergies in the energy sector. As the shale revolution continues to reshape global energy dynamics, US-Gulf relations are poised to undergo further evolution, characterized by a blend of competition, cooperation, and strategic adaptation. Navigating this transformation requires a nuanced understanding of the interplay between energy, geopolitics, and economic interdependencies and proactive efforts to align national interests and foster sustainable partnerships.

Environmental Considerations: Challenges and Criticisms

The rapidly growing production of energy, particularly shale oil and gas extraction development, has posed serious environmental considerations that have come to the forefront when discussing threats and criticisms. One of the most prominent issues is predicated on the possible environmental consequences of hydraulic fracturing, popularly known as fracking. This method of extracting natural gas and oil from the earth's crust is very deep and has raised serious concerns about water quality and pollution as well as seismic activities. It is contended that the water and chemical components released during the production process endanger surrounding aquifers, surface water, and ecosystems, as well as the methane released during the process endangers the global climate through greenhouse gas emissions. In addition, the disposal of wastewater and the prospect of pollution of underground water resources are receiving more attention from regulators and the public vicinity. The impact of America's increasing energy dominance is causing more international concern, especially regarding climate change. The efforts of America to achieve independence in terms of energy and become a net exporter of energy resources come with the additional challenge of having to extract and move fossil fuels in a more environmentally friendly manner.

The new focus on environmental sustainability in diplomacy and geopolitics relates to how America is viewed as an energy superpower and to unilateral and multilateral deals. Also, the environmental concerns associated with energy dominance highlight the need for innovations and cleaner resources, which increase investments in renewables and advancements in efficiency. In other words, decision-makers need to consider the economic advantages of energy production while considering the responsibility of managing environmental impacts associated with ecological balance. Addressing these issues requires an integrated system of scientific research, industrial practices, and policy regulations to achieve sustainable energy solutions alongside environmental conservation efforts in a changing world.

Diplomatic Leverage: Energy as a Foreign Policy Tool

In the broader context of international relations, energy-producing states have vital control levers due to their oil and gas reserves, which can be the strongest diplomatic weapon. Considering this dynamic, their foreign policy goals of making allies, strengthening friendships, and putting pressure on opponents can be met. Changes to these relationships can be constructed considering the control of oil and gas reserves. The US has a history of shaping diplomatic relationships and furthering overseas interests during conflicts through intently adopting practices of power relations. It preaches policy and ideology to energy-rich countries using this power and position. It tries to establish alliances that encourage a drop in spice-for-fuel trade and foster stability as regions of vital importance turn hostile. As a case in point, these relations go into oblivion when Trump's period is brought into foray, where he doggedly pushed for energy dominance to be explicated as part of the foreign diplomacy agenda. Oil and natural gas gave US energy-political relations with resource-dependent countries a new approach. So, from that side of the subject, the strategy of the world's superpower got freedom in the gauge, and conditions were adequately set to achieve greater political gains.

Likewise, oil-rich countries like Saudi Arabia and Russia have leveraged their immense oil reserves to gain geopolitical influence. Using energy exports for diplomacy has helped these countries build alliances, politically dominate, and gain economically. At the same time, there are worries about the possible weaponisation of energy for geopolitical reasons. Such measures could spark market uncertainty, increase global confrontations, and possibly weaken global energy security. Additionally, using fossil fuels for state diplomacy poses a problem of international concern and calls for a shift to renewable energy sources. While trying to find the nexus between energy relations and diplomacy, it is crucial to determine the moral boundaries and impact posed by weaponising energy resources for policies regarding international relations.

Advancements in the extraction of energy resources over the last few decades have modernised the entire world energy system. The latest discoveries in the USA regarding psychic stimulation and side drilling have led to an economic boost. This, in turn, has aided the US in the race towards energy self-sufficiency and impacted global alliances and geopolitics.

Moreover, new technologies have been developed that allow for the possibility of unlocking traditional oil and gas reserves alongside both new and existing market competitors. Integrating artificial intelligence and data science in resource search and drilling enhances efficacy and accuracy, resulting in increased profits and reduced costs. Moreover, harvesting renewable resources like solar and wind has also received a lot of focus, promoting further diversification of the global energy mix. On the other hand, the evolving environment poses challenges—environmental impact, regulatory systems, and infrastructure development continue to be very important issues. It is necessary to adopt proactive policies and invest in research and development to take full advantage of the risks that come with new technologies. With the continuous change of markets, shifts in demand and supply dynamics, collaboration, and strategic flexibility among industry stakeholders will be vital to leverage the benefits of these pace-setting technologies. The balance between advanced extraction methods and environmental protection is critical in achieving more sustainable energy in the future. Governments, industry, and academic institutions must work together to address the energy market's complicated aspects and at the intersection of technology, policy, and economics that will impact the energy system for decades.

Technological Advancements in Energy Extraction

The shifting scenario of energy markets around the globe has led to both opportunities and challenges for OPEC member states. This has prompted the organisation to contemplate policies that are meant to ensure its relevance and control for a longer duration. In response to changing market dynamics and geopolitical pressures, OPEC is undertaking adaptive steps to preserve its central role in controlling the production and pricing of oil in the market. These initiatives are being undertaken alongside changes in market conditions. Above all, these adaptive measures focus on collaboration within and outside the organisation. OPEC and several non-member producers must improve their relationships to strengthen their supply influence, having previously founded a co-operation alliance with Russia. OPEC seeks to strengthen its joint leverage on the world's oil supply levels and maintain steady prices during instability through these agreements. OPEC has further enhanced its internal systems control to improve responsiveness to decisions relating to activities in the market. Encouraging agreement of national interests and, consequently, production levels within the organisation is one necessary step that has been taken. Enhancing cooperation with important nations that consume oil and sponsors from other international bodies to solve problems of interest and sustain the market has also been the primary goal set by OPEC.

With a shift in the adoption of renewable energy sources and a focus on cleaner technology solutions, OPEC countries seem to be taking proactive steps towards innovation and diversifying investment opportunities. Also, integrating sustainable development policies concerning environmental preservation into OPEC's operational framework reflects highly strategic planning towards future shifts in energy demand and climate oversight. Lastly, OPEC is trying to manage the complexities of modern energy geopolitics through proactive measures, adaptive responses, and complex planning schemes. Through innovation, active collaboration, and strategic foresight, OPEC seeks to overcome immediate challenges and establish robust relevance in the future global energy system.

OPEC Reactions and Adaptive Strategies

To guide the expenses incurred on our basic limited budget, the expected patterns of economic advancement after comprehensive drug manufacturing processes will gather all qualitative attributes together while also incorporating spiritual progress, especially considering that one and a half lakh jobs created could be linked to operational tasks in the US post prospecting and recording of insights from the bloodstream, as well as through channels such as specialised forums. The newcomer nations like Russia will see certain resources emerge prominently in a year and a half after declaring their developmental intentions in illuminated sectors pursuing "10-15" billion targets. The demand for distribution of loans related to their sectors is heightened during transitions from agriculture to energy with an increase in efforts towards functional sanitation, allied with contracts enabling alternative solutions in the mechanical drug manufacturing industry, while also addressing counterproductive scenarios, iridian controversies and any pertaining exigencies to clarify the correspondence therein.

Renewable resources are now classified as sustainable energy technologies and pose challenges and opportunities for developing states, especially the Gulf States. The shifts in policies regarding climate change mitigation mark a noteworthy turning point for America, the EU, and developing economies. With states acknowledging the possible sustainable energy resources within their land, paradigm shifts towards energy markets in parts of North Africa and the merchantable resources of western country blocks have emerged. These involvements greatly benefit the Gulf States as they seek to diversify their fossil fuel economies. Adapting to such new long-term trends is and should be part of the strategic focus for the Gulf States. Developing and implementing sustainable energy initiatives require considerable expenditure in research, infrastructure, policy frameworks, and international collaborations. Alongside this transition, long-term trends indicate a change in global consumer preferences, regulatory policies, and geopolitical relationships that will further redefine the future energy balance.

Taking proactive action against technological constraints, market instability, and geopolitical uncertainties is pivotal in moving towards a sustainable energy future. Furthermore, the need to plan well ahead in adopting these sustainable energy solutions requires the elimination of potential disruptions to deliver reliable energy supply. The Gulf States hold remarkable reserves of wealth and human resources and stand to gain from placing their expertise in the energy domain, thus becoming primary actors that will shape the future trajectories of the region. They have opportunities to aid in these transitions and boost their global standing by adopting responsible energy policies that reduce the environmental consequences of energy consumption. Moreover, these trends correspond with changing long-term consumer attitudes, the need to respond to global climate commitments, and shifts in supply chains, thus bringing the Gulf States to the epicentre of changes in the world's energy system. To summarise, the drive towards sustainable energy and response to long-term trends will define regional and global energy dominance. The Gulf States can leverage their assets for enhanced relevance in the new energy order while advancing resilience and sustainability in the world's energy system.

8

Transactional Diplomacy

Demanding Returns from Regional Allies

Overview of Transactional Diplomacy: Definitions and Origins

At its core, transactional diplomacy is as old as the world itself. It stems from the very fabric of international relations. States have engaged in transactions—for security, economic, or even diplomatic reasons. This recurring theme is pivotal to understanding global alliances and historical power shifts. The most primitive forms of transactional diplomacy include ancient treaties, military alliances, and trade agreements, which have both positively and negatively defined global politics. Modern forms of diplomacy stem from the evolution (or rather devolution) of U.S. foreign policies. With the U.S. being a hyperpower for so long, it relied on transactional diplomacy to consolidate power and strengthen national interests.

Furthermore, it became a superpower by establishing complex alliances and creating impenetrable spheres of influence. In arms, aid, diplomacy, and even trade negotiations, the U.S. is perceived as upholding dependent relationships with numerous nations worldwide while extending open arms to others (hence the term 'superpower'). The nature of U.S. foreign policies causes a shift in the balance of power in regions where national interests are undermined. The cornerstone of transactional diplomacy is simpler – receiving tangible rewards through diplomatic exchanges.

In addition, changes in the global distribution of power, new technologies, and evolving risks and opportunities in international relations have influenced the use of transactional diplomacy. The development of this type of diplomacy highlights the balance between geopolitics' strategic realities and statecraft's needs. In other words, transactional diplomacy is a strategy that acts flexibly to achieve specific goals in the conduct of foreign policy.

Historical Context: Precedents in US Foreign Policy

The term' transactional diplomacy' describes a form of diplomacy in which specific results are sought through deals and negotiations with foreign allies. Such diplomacy has been evident in American foreign relations. American presidents have always interacted with foreign nations in a practical way that strives to receive something of value in return. An illustrative case is the 1803 Louisiana Purchase where President Thomas Jefferson entered into a remarkable deal with France. In this transaction, the United States acquired a vast territory from France, effectively doubling the size of the country. This type of purchase is often referred to as a manner of expansion that provides economic opportunities. The U.S. Marshall Plan after the Second World War was, in its essence, such a remarkable diplomatic purchase when America provided financial assistance to rebuild Western Europe's economy, so that peace and stability could be maintained, and the spread of communism was countered. The balance between the help being offered and the American interests being served captures the essence of this historic initiative. Another important precedent relates to Nixon's administration and the policy of détente with the Soviet Union during the Cold War. The US sought to reduce tensions and achieve highly defined strategic objectives through cooperative arms control treaties. Such policies embody the more evident forms of transactional diplomacy.

Moreover, the Camp David Accords in 1978, which President Jimmy Carter brokered, marked a significant transactionally oriented milestone when peace was negotiated between Israel and Egypt, underscoring the use of rewards and compromises to achieve goals. These illustrations highlight the frequency and impact of such diplomacy on American global relations. Developing such diplomatic strategies in America's foreign policy is insightful amidst current concerns, revealing the intricate possibilities of diplomacy based on calculated exchanges versus conventional relations.

Strategic Goals: Aligning Diplomatic Transactions with National Interests

As a branch of international relations, the United States implements transactional diplomacy by aligning diplomatic exchanges with national interests. This strategic alignment ensures that diplomatic transactions promote, at a minimum, the country's security, economic interests, and geopolitical standing. The analytic design of strategic goals within this scope requires a balance between sought constructive results and mapping out the delicate balance of national interests with the global arena, instilling confidence in its effectiveness.

United States security policies and those of its allies are comparatively analysed alongside a country's geopolitical strategy to form a national interest. This integration enables forging strong partnerships and alliances that enhance regional security and stifle security threats of common concern. Diplomatic transactions are meticulously fine-tuned to secure pledges from allies that add to collective defence capabilities and act as force multipliers to emerging security concerns. To balance the security interests of allied nations, the US attempts to strengthen its strategic position and reduce security weaknesses.

Furthermore, as obtaining national priorities through transactional diplomacy also involves procuring economic opportunities and mutual benefits, it can also be examined in this context. Transactions in diplomacy aim to create favourable conditions for business, investment, and technology activities, enhancing economic development, innovation, and employment. The alignment of such transactions with national interests requires using economic cooperation to support American enterprises, increase their market penetration, and obtain favourable conditions of trade. The United States attempts to deepen the control of its economy by incorporating economic considerations into political relations and counterbalance the economy by exploiting national purposes with economic opportunities abroad.

Moreover, the strategic integration of diplomacy with national interests goes to soft power exploitation and the advocacy of democracy and human rights. Diplomacy is designed to motivate compliance with democratic governance, human dignity, and freedom, thus forming dispositions which enhance American ideals. Promotive transactions by the United States seek to shape the prevailing international climate into one which supports democracy, the rule of law, and respect for human rights, thereby fortifying the foundation for a peaceful and prosperous world order. In other words, within unilateral diplomacy, there are multidimensional approaches intended to pursue national interests, which are, in fact, a fully packed agenda on the international scene.

Regional Power Dynamics: Expectations from Middle Eastern Allies

As the geopolitical map of the Middle East shifts, the United States faces a multifaceted challenge of an intricate regional power structure and alliance. Middle Eastern allies are pivotal to the balance of power and execution of the key diplomatic initiatives. Their expectations include political, economic, and security aspects requiring deeper and more sophisticated engagement.

Associated with American interests, the U.S.-Middle East relationships primarily focus on regional stability, counterterrorism, and the containment of rivals. Nevertheless, each ally has priorities and perspectives shaped by history, domestic politics, and aspirations of being a regional power. For example, Saudi Arabia and Israel expect some degree of unconditional support against shared rivals while being allowed to pursue their national interests. In contrast, new regional leaders such as the United Arab Emirates seek to increase their influence and diversify strategic partnerships, thus creating collaborative and competitive opportunities for the United States.

The expectations of American allies in the Middle East also include economic cooperation and development assistance. To enhance their global competitiveness, these countries strive to modernise their economies and seek technological investment, trade agreements, and even research partnerships with the United States. At the same time, these countries expect that the United States will play a stabilising role in the challenges of regional economics (oil price volatility or global market disruptions). The transformation of the Middle East into a sustainable growth innovation hub aligns with the United States' vision for the region, reinforcing the need to meet the economic expectations of its allies.

Given the region's prevailing acute instability and security risks, the security outlook constitutes the backbone of American relations with Middle Eastern allies. These allies need to receive strong security guarantees, such as military assistance, defence partnership, and intelligence support, to deal with the threats of terrorism, transnational insurgencies, and destabilising influences. To achieve these security arrangements, however, the right balance needs to be struck between increasing their ability and avoiding creating too many unintended consequences that destabilise the entire region.

The United States must exercise diplomacy, long-term planning, and flexibility when dealing with Middle Eastern allies since their multifaceted expectations require profound attention. To nurture sustainable relationships and achieve goals, it is critical to comprehend the expectations within their historical, cultural, and geopolitical layers. The shifting balance of power in the region requires prudent policies that advance mutual goals while honouring the independence and self-determination of Middle Eastern allies.

Economic Leverage: Utilising Trade and Investment Policies

Within the broad domain of diplomacy, using trade and advancing investment policies rank highly in maintaining good relations. Strasbourg could annex Hamburgh diplomatically because of the economic penalties they weakened in Strasbourg. America's relationship with Mexico improved immensely owing to America's Investment Initiatives. These measures give room to restrain a partner. These policies give governments negotiable leverage, ensuring better economic relationships and policies. It makes it easy to get cooperation from the partner such that they comply, and basing the relationship on controlled behaviours makes the outcomes general and long-lasting. Everything works with a guided understanding of the economy and the political objectives set for different states when needed. The alignment of economics towards political objectives helps to achieve thorough cooperation without causing economic friction. Protection policies grant security to the nations as relations are made dynamic. Committing defence forces and integrating trade serves to alter security weak trade-despot approaches. From this, partner nations get great command of the economy while helping change the terms of partnered reliance on

outsiders, securing advanced boost to productivity, hence changing various strategies that make the economic policies more rev-
enue-generating for areas obedient to the well-off.

Fine-tuning trade and investment offers to meet particular requirements while motivating compliance with broader organisational goals, which is difficult and complex. However, the responsible use of economic power requires caution regarding its effects
on global markets and the overall financial equilibrium. Foresight
and control of these consequences are essential to maintaining balance without destabilising the system. Ultimately, the greatest skill
in using economic tools for diplomacy is developing relationships
that harness economic growth with strategic resources and are
programmable for an easier life. The relationships based on strong
positions can identify enduring cooperative projects with the help
of sustained efforts to support alliances that promote regional and
global unity.

Security Commitments: Linking Military Aid to Compliance

In relations between states, security commitments capture the
defining feature of any alliance between countries. Historically, the balance of power and military assistance has been a hall-
mark of United States policy towards its allies in the Middle East.
This model contains elements of diplomacy and army cooperation
alongside the formulation of policies. These actions cannot be
defined only as gestures; rather, they can be regarded as an appreciation of common security risks, threat perception, defence vulnerabilities, and the need to work together. Thus, linking military aid
to compliance becomes one of the most important determinants

of the efficiency and accountability of such alliances.

The task of linking military aid to compliance standards requires one to carefully draw the line on both incentives and punishment. In this context, compliance refers to the recipient's adherence to the agreed terms of engagement, which may include respect for human rights, commitment to non-proliferation, and regional stability efforts. In this manner, aid is also bound to these parameters, which results in the possibility of efficiency at the federal level, tempered by the responsible action avoidance of resource redirection towards mutual interests. Such a policy would create an environment conducive to behaviour modification while crafting punitive measures for those who step out of the defined standards.

Regardless, the connection between military assistance and compliance has its issues. This relates to sovereignty, domestic politics, and the sovereign authority of states to determine their security policies. Combining the need for system-wide security with the danger of fragmentation calls for practical balance. Also, dealing with the changing geopolitical environment, which may involve shifts in power dynamics or the emergence of new threats, requires responsiveness in assessing the relevance of the agreements and their adjustments to current security conditions.

Linking compliance to military aid is not just about forming trust, it's about sustaining it. This trust is the foundation of responsible defence cooperation, which in turn is the key to achieving and maintaining regional stability. It's equally important to sustain a constructive dialogue to prevent and resolve issues, disengage, and recapture the essence of the engagement, if need be.

When analysing security commitments and military aid, the region's historical and strategic frameworks and dynamic threats and opportunities are always present. Even though this approach poses an underlying challenge, it emphasises the extent of US involvement in the region, demonstrating its desire for deeper relationships through shared security interests and responsibilities.

Diplomatic Challenges: Negotiating Complex Bilateral Agreements

Creating complex international agreements in transactions-based diplomacy is multifaceted and presents countless hurdles that require specialised diplomatic skills and advanced planning. These agreements require negotiations between two sovereign states with conflicting national, geopolitical, and economic interests. Achieving a consensus requires a balanced approach where attention is paid to the details, and there is the comprehension of expectation management and negotiation balance.

Perhaps the most focused diplomatic attempts are spent on merging the bilateral treaty with the priorities of both parties in a strategically beneficial way over an extended period. This means that, at a minimum, several meetings and discussions are conducted to ensure that the agreed-upon terms have a favourable impact on foreign policy objectives, regional integration, and collective security. Usually, the balancing act requires navigating intricate geopolitical shifting tides, enduring historical grievances, and checking the support or lack thereof, from domestic politics regarding the treaty.

Moreover, dealing with trade deficits, entrepreneurial rights, and convergence of regulations when striking deals is not the only complexity faced when drawing bilateral contracts; all these issues must be resolved simultaneously. Such detail requires thorough research, expert analyses, and flexibility in accommodating diverse economic systems and sets of laws and regulations. Forging an agreement that fulfils the prerequisites of an enduring shift while addressing the disparity problem among participating countries is more than a challenge; it is a problem needing advanced knowledge of international relations, trade, and economics.

Managing sensitivity concerning culture and socio-political issues is not just crucial, it's a fundamental aspect of dealing with complex bilateral agreements. Culture and societal norms often play a significant role in the dynamics of any society, influencing the decision-making and implementation phases of the contracts being signed by diplomats. A deep understanding and diplomats who treat these issues with great care and respect using soft-spoken engagement and cultural nuances build rapport and trust with their opposing parties, highlighting the importance of these qualities in international diplomacy.

Managing compliance and enforcement about bilateral agreements is not just a complex task, it's a delicate balancing act. Striking the right balance between control and sovereignty, autonomy, self-governance, or jurisdiction is crucial. This balance is necessary to address intricate issues concerning the enforcement of stringent mechanisms to monitor adherence to the terms of the agreement and the resolution of disputes. Each stage of the negotiation must delineate unyielding respect for legal jurisdiction and balance control, emphasising the importance of fairness and respect in international agreements.

In conclusion, overcoming the challenges of multifaceted bilateral agreements requires understanding the strategic details of communication, multifaceted diplomacy, multidisciplinary negotiations, and cultural nuances alongside economic and geopolitical factors. Meeting these challenges strengthens bilateral relationships, increases understanding and deeper insight, and achieves common goals in an increasingly dynamic world.

Critiques and Controversies: Ethical and Practical Concerns

One primary form of transactional diplomacy in international relationships has drawn considerable controversy regarding ethics and practicality. Critics contend that a transactional approach to diplomacy neglects vital overarching interests and strategically weakens lasting friendships, treating relationships as mere commodities to be bought and sold for short-term profit. From an ethical viewpoint, imposing conditions that aid and support must pass through gates tends to be seen as coercive, undermining mutual respect or shared goals and breaching universal principles of cooperation. In addition, using economic or military aid to achieve certain policy goals brings to light other critical questions of powerful nations' broader moral obligations toward global stability and development. Equally important is the transactional nature of this approach, which draws attention to equity and fairness issues within these relations, particularly in dealings with politically weaker partners. Moreover, some of these countries tend to create dependency or an authoritarian posture as they attempt to comply with the conditions in place to gain essential support. From a practical perspective, these critics point out that transactional diplomacy may result in backlash from perceived rigid and self-serving associates. Allies may foster feelings of resentment and resistance.

Such dynamics may erode trust and collaboration, diminishing the efficacy of relations between the two parties and adding difficulty in understanding the region. Furthermore, the strategic nature behind interactions where agreements are exchanged between parties gives little room for diplomacy. It may impede responsiveness to emerging geopolitical issues, which is likely counterproductive regarding proactive measures that could have been taken. Another issue of concern focuses on the implications of transactional demands on broader international standards and the state's credibility in enforcing such standards, as imposing unreasonable unilateral demands risks anger and weakens the moral standing essential to lead effectively on an international scale. In attempting to advance these criticisms and controversies, it becomes clear that we seek balance in applying transactional diplomacy, transforming it from a perceived blunt tool into one that promotes policies aligned with shared interests delineated by ethical conduct and real partnership.

Case Studies: Successful and Unsuccessful Transactions

It is important to explore particular case studies that showcase both successful and unsuccessful transactions to analyse diplomacy in the Middle East, which requires diving into the dynamics of transactional diplomacy. From multiple diplomatic transactions undertaken within the US, there seems to be a pattern where allied countries within the region showcase different results and consequences.

One remarkable example of successful transactional diplomacy is the Camp David Accords 1978. During this time, US President Jimmy Carter hosted the historic Israel-Egypt peace talks, in which both nations came up with a peace treaty to resolve conflicts that existed for decades and would become the basis for future friendly relations between them. Another example would be the Clinton

Parameters during the 2000 Camp David Summit. There was intensive US involvement, with efforts directed towards devising a comprehensive peace settlement for Israel and Palestine. This depicts a highly intensive, or high-risk, transactional approach that ultimately did not succeed.

On the other hand, an example of how transactional diplomacy was applied unsuccessfully was after the Iraq War. Iraq post-war continued to deal with internal conflict, ethnic violence, and political disarray despite the US pouring military and economic resources into it. This exposes blind spots relating to applying transactional diplomacy for nation-building. Moreover, the complicated talks surrounding the Iran nuclear deal and the withdrawal from the deal under Trump capture the intense and rapid shifts in the political context that the undertaking or expiration of these fundamental agreements creates within the changing geopolitical framework.

The case studies highlight the multifaceted dynamics concerning power, interests, and chronological periods in the Middle East, revealing important nuances related to transactional diplomacy. They expose the intricacies involved in the negotiations and execution of diplomatic transactions and the interplay of immediate value versus strategic imperatives over time. These case studies illustrate the ethical, political, and practical issues that frame such interactions. Such case studies are relevant for policy and diplomatic initiatives in the Middle East with the engagement of multi-layered diplomacy.

Future Outlook: Sustaining Partnership through Mutual Benefit

The viability of future diplomatic relations between the US and other Middle Eastern countries hinges on the countries' sustained mutual benefits and shared interests in a constantly shifting political climate. In contrast to advancing transactional diplomacy, the enduring partnership approach is based on strategic multidimensional relations and joint conflict resolution.

To begin with, recalibration entails focusing on equitable bargains that tackle each side's primary needs and priorities. This means moving from a myopic view focused on immediate benefits to a wider approach that incorporates economic development, security cooperation, and regional stability. Aligning objectives and acknowledging the intricacies within the region increases the likelihood of sustainable collective mutual benefit.

In addition, the future of partnership in the Middle East region requires the United States to actively commit to inclusivity and multilateralism geared towards the region's diversifying needs. The US must find cooperative approaches that aid in turning the hopes of all stakeholders into reality. This serves the enduring partnership by preventing the system from fracturing under external or internal tensions.

Moreover, developing and maintaining sustainable partnerships requires an acute awareness of shifting global power relations and other factors of international development. The US and its Middle Eastern allies need to adjust their frameworks of cooperation in relation to the world's multifaceted problems, such as climate change, new technologies, and non-state actors. With adequate expertise and resources, the partnership can be positioned as a competent defender of the global agenda.

Regarding strategic foresight, the emphasis on mutual trust, transparency, and systematic communication cannot be overstated. Partnership relations underpinned by respect and open dialogue at all levels are vital for the success of any cooperative venture. Such principles greatly improve the ability to withstand challenges, navigate disagreements, and bolster the strength and durability of the alliance.

Given the need to adapt alongside political shifts, the expectation stems from focusing on sustaining the partnership through mutual benefits directed towards shared goals. Understanding that the geopolitical reality is ever-changing, the US and regional partners must cooperate proactively. Strategies focused on refining defined objectives will ensure the partnership remains relevant and beneficial in the years to come.

9

Military Restraint

Redefining America's Security Role in the Region

The Tradition of Military Presence

The history of the American military presence worldwide is linked to its growing economic and political influence, with military bases established post-World War II in North Africa, Europe, and Southeast Asia while extending alliances with Japan and South Korea. Collier contends that America primarily adopts a militaristic approach to international relations, utilising its extensive control over forces and economic resources to maintain order and stability. Centre towards Vermont, the Aryan Nations' former leader Hayden has actively promoted white supremacy and Christian Identity movements across America—alongside Operation Red Dog and other minor conflicts instigated by United States mercenaries. The foundation of the United States Navy during the 1780s was relied upon to tighten control and encourage trade and commerce with separate countries.

The tradition of American military presence in the Middle East is deeply rooted in the region's geopolitical dynamics, which are responsible for its national development, security imperatives, and global strategic intricacies. After the conclusion of World War II, the United States, as a superpower, gradually deepened its involvement in the Middle East, influenced by the region's unique geopolitical factors. These factors, such as the strategic importance of the region's energy resources and the complex web of alliances and conflicts, have shaped American policy in the region, particularly in terms of security and stability.

The historical context of America's military ventures fully came into focus in the period of the Middle Region, which was crucial in the projection of power and continued to develop. The sub-kingdom coalitions and other Indo-European conflicts paved the way for a military partnership with China, which was centred on the Middle Kingdom and fuelled China's foreign policy. As a result, the Two Super Powers had to ensure Stability during the pre-mer of 1979 and afterwards until the mid-1990s American reign and ensure power in every region in the Middle East after The Amalgamated Gulf War.

The Persian Gulf incidents further developed substantial defensive strategies to maintain the Gulf War Coalition alongside the Establishment of Forced Brezstrocy in post-Afghan America; using fallacies to claim them as aggressors marked the rest of the militarisation drives.

The safeguard of critical maritime chokepoints like the Strait of Hormuz, combined with the need to counter international terrorism, has reinforced the importance of a permanent American military presence in the Middle East. This presence, in turn, is explained by the United States's more expansive and long-term strategic considerations, such as managing the spread of the proliferation of weapons of mass destruction, protecting free trade, and assuring reliable allies in the region about US commitment to their defence. Thus, studying chronologically the history of America's military engagements in the Middle East reveals important insights regarding the constantly evolving influences that have shaped and perpetuated this engagement, as well as served to contextualise the dominant influences for assessing alterations in defence planning.

Historical Context: America's Role in Middle Eastern Security

American participation in maintaining security in the Middle East has a multifaceted history that began in the early 20th century. With the conclusion of World War II, the United States had emerged as a superpower and increasingly focused its energy on the international politics of the Middle East. The foundation of Israel in 1948 was a major turning point in American involvement with the region, deepening entwined conflict and alliances that shape American policy to this day.

During the Cold War, the Middle East became an ideological and strategic battleground for the United States and the Soviet Union. The United States, in its efforts to prevent the spread of communism and protect access to critical energy supplies, adopted the Eisenhower Doctrine. This doctrine, which was a cornerstone of American foreign policy in the region, fostered strong alliances with countries like Iran and Saudi Arabia, solidifying US influence over regional security and shaping the geopolitical landscape of the

Middle East.

The events surrounding the Iranian Revolution of 1979, along with the subsequent hostage crisis, were a turning point that altered American views towards the Middle East. These events caused the US to change and reconsider its alliances with and interventions in the region. The Gulf War from 1990 to 1991 further cemented US policies focused on maintaining stability around the free flow of oil, resulting in a heightened military presence in the area and a reevaluation of its role in the region's security dynamics.

After the events of September 11, 2001, the US initiated the Global War on Terror, which was marked by military actions in Afghanistan and Iraq. These wars highlighted the difficulties and intricacies surrounding Middle Eastern interventions, forcing the US to reconsider the scope of its involvement and the role it aimed to fulfil regarding the region's security.

The more recent emergence of global non-state actors, shifts in energy resource distribution, and new geopolitical tension hotspots have all contributed to an adjustment in the way America historically approached security in the Middle East. In the context of everything stated previously, we explore how America's deep-rooted history continues to shape and redefine the country's strategy in the region.

Assessing Current Capabilities and Deployments

The evaluation of active capabilities and deployments is a complex task that requires a deep understanding of the geopolitical environment and the security challenges facing the Middle East. Here, we analyse the military arsenal and the strategic posture of American forces in the region considering both the contemporary and historical contexts. It is important to understand that the employment of military capabilities goes beyond simply achieving a favourable potential balance. Efficiency, interoperability, adaptability, and precision all play significant roles. Therefore, I will cover all relevant supplementary assets including forward operating bases, logistics, airlift, and sealift. Particular focus will be placed on policy alignment and initiatives to ensure interagency synergy related to diplomatic efforts and overall regional security. Furthermore, the analysis will assess the emissions gap and countering asymmetric threats, cyber vulnerabilities, unconventional weapon proliferation, and the effectiveness of current deployments. From the operational perspective of force dynamics and projection constructs, this assessment seeks to evaluate effectiveness and explore strategic recalibration and optimisation options.

It is crucial to understand the regional alliances and relationships that support American deployments, which include host nation support, joint exercises, and collective security arrangements. Moreover, the recent change in the geopolitical landscape, including the withdrawal from some theatres and the concentration of presence into primary areas of interest, will be analysed regarding its impact on deterrence, crisis response, and force sustainment. The study will also focus on the contribution of intelligence, surveillance, reconnaissance, and other associated activities to maintaining full motion and situational awareness. Finally, examining operational support, maintenance of strategic assets, and social human capital components like staff sentiment, operational readiness, and attrition will highlight the multidisciplinary nature of this assessment. We aim to articulate a more sophisticated and balanced view of the available military capabilities and deployments to refine the approach towards America's security posture in the region.

The Pivot Towards Strategic Restraint

The United States has evolved and continues to evolve its approach to the Middle East as a region of strategic interest, which now seems to be adopting a strategic restraint approach. This marks a reconsidered understanding of the United States' foreign policy militaristic vision because it acknowledges that there are intricate and nuanced realities that require deeper understanding. Strategic restraint does not mean the unilateral withdrawal of forces; instead, it highlights an adjustment to the American security posture in the region.

This change towards strategic restraint is guided by an understanding of the negative consequences of extended military involvement. In today's world, where threats are asymmetric, multifaceted, and multilayered, the advantages associated with imposing an extensive military presence tend to be exceedingly dwarfed by disproportionate risks and expenditures. By adopting strategic restraint, the United States endeavours to pursue its interests and foster stabilisation much more sustainably and effectively.

The pivot is primarily centred around diplomatic and coalition-building initiatives with regional partner states. The US seeks to promote partnerships with important allies and even key stakeholders in the Middle East because, about security, they expect that division of labour and shared responsibilities will be crucial in the success of a strategic posture. This sustains a focus on mobilising resources to establish security frameworks and coalitions for collective action, demonstrating cooperation to counteract a shared danger and achieve a common goal.

Furthermore, the strategic restraint move allows recalibration in resource and capability allocation. This shift does not only focus on a military approach but rather on a combination of statecraft, including economic, diplomatic, and technological investment. With this multifaceted approach, the US can advance its national security interests without imposing active, long-term military deployments that are strategically harmful.

On the other hand, a shift towards strategic restraint also requires some degree of careful handling of the embedded issues and sacrifices that need to be made. Demonstrating resolve without showing weakness needs sharp diplomacy, a clear strategy, or slight foresight. Also, strategic restraint must ensure that it does not invite an increase in boldness from adversaries or lower the trust of regional allies.

Strategic restraint as an initiative, unlike military action, advances 'strategic agility' and a responsive American security approach in the Middle East, considering long-lasting American interests and influence in mitigating potential risks in the region. It showcases the adoption of new, emerging American policies that seek to promote lasting stability in the region.

Balancing Power: Coalition Building with Regional Partners

In the progression of the Middle Eastern geopolitical spectrum, coalition building became an essential aspect of providing balance and stabilising the region. The focus of the chapter is on the complex nature of forming and maintaining alliances with strategic regional partners to achieve shared security goals. The United States, employing a diverse strategy, aims to build support from core allies while simultaneously adjusting to the changing shape of the regional political landscape.

While an intricate network of interests unfolds, the USA faces the problem of integrating differing national frameworks into a single system. Using diplomatic avenues and security treaties, the US seeks to expand its influence with Israel, Saudi Arabia, and the Gulf Cooperation Council (GCC) states in coordinated efforts. These partnerships, militarily and economically, contain common enemies and open possibilities for a joint response to new dangers.

In addition, coalition building involves working across splitting social fault lines, which entails a sophisticated shift in power positioning in the region. The US attempts to create lasting sponsored collaborations towards the south border of Canada with advanced defence technologies to enhance the US security framework through increasing joint military drills and interoperability of the participating nations to form a united defence strategy. The cumulative result improves local defence capacity while deepening the common will to defend local order against reasonable changes.

Finally, creating strategic alliances rests heavily on the need for burden-sharing and resource maximisation. Through joint defence and capacity-building measures, the United States and its regional allies establish a cooperative network that optimally integrates operational efficiency and crisis response capabilities. Additionally, the diversification of military infrastructure and intelligence-sharing systems enhances the coalition's adaptability and responsiveness, creating an all-encompassing security network.

Subsequent chapters make it increasingly clear that building these coalitions strengthens the regional security framework and enhances more broad strategic objectives. The added value of aligned partnerships expands beyond the conventional focus of security to include economic relations, counterterrorism, and resilience to outside pressure. Strengthening regional partnerships allows the United States to adjust its approach towards the Middle

East by softening its security focus to a more integrated approach that strengthens its ability to confront complex problems.

Essentially, coalition building embodies the recasting of America's strategic footprint in the region, moving beyond military presence to a more fluid collective security model. With persistent involvement and carefully calculated diplomatic manoeuvres, the US and its allies in the region actively develop a system that fosters integration, stability, and strength, thereby crafting a powerful architecture to defend shared interests and influence the geopolitical landscape of the Middle East.

Evaluating the Economic Costs of Sustained Engagement

Within the context of the United States' rethinking of its geopolitical security dynamics in the Middle East, one of the critical elements is the economic burden of military engagement over a sustained period. There has been considerable controversy and debate surrounding the enormous financial costs associated with the military's active presence in a particular region. This purpose tries to analyse further the details of this economic factor. It includes the analysis regarding direct expenditures of military actions, like costs incurred for deployment, maintenance of bases, and logistical aids. In addition, there is also a great need to study the budgetary contours of additional military expenditures in the long term, particularly during the shifting international priorities, domestic policies, and imperatives. Besides direct costs, there are other underlying economic components that require attention. These underlying components include, but are not limited to, opportunity costs with regard to expenditure and resource concentration in the

Middle East region and the adverse effect on its economic and investment stability. A more comprehensive examination of engagement's impact reveals the military's involvement in the dynamics of the energy sector and the effects on international trade and commerce, which are all essential for formulating an understanding of ongoing military involvement. The complicated phenomena of economic mutual dependence, where the economies of the US and the Middle East are intertwined, alongside the possible rivalry over resources highlight the importance of this assessment.

Aside from the monetary aspects, the costs involved with the regional partners' enduring effort engagement are also an economic factor. The US shifts its strategy as it engages the region differently, focusing on these finances, workforce, and capital expenditures. I will attempt to outline the specific economic factors detailing them so that this analysis contributes to the discussion regarding redefining America's role and security posture in the Middle East.

The Role of Technology and Remote Engagement

The sword has two edges, and in this case, the United States facing security issues in the Middle East has motivated them to develop UAVs, cyber technologies, and discipline within remote warfare. Along with other technologies, these advancements have greatly changed the operational environment of warfare. However, remote technology allows the US to enhance its defence capabilities further.

One of the most lethal concerns of warfare is the loss of life, particularly among American soldiers. Warfare technology, such as drones that can be used for surveillance or air strikes while operated from a distance, are game changers. They drastically reduce poor soldier casualty rates. The aforementioned is the lowest promise member set under remote warfare. Drones and intelligence from satellites reduce violence among US forces. The capacity to accurately pinpoint and neutralise specific threats while restricting collateral damage has evident positive consequences for humanitarian efforts and can assist in diminishing hostile views of US military activity in the Middle East.

In addition to the combat domain, the United States exercises advanced cyber offensive and defensive capabilities. Modern-day conflicts have shifted cyberspace into a more prominent battleground, and cyber warfare can extemporaneously destroy an enemy's communications, infrastructure, and even political system. Therefore, influencing a region through cyber warfare has become a critical method for altering power dynamics in that region.

However, the ease of remote access enabled by technology raises new ethical and legal questions. The employment of unmanned aerial vehicles and cyber weaponry is especially problematic regarding responsibility, collateral damage, and international standards of law. These problems are challenges integrating America's military might into the region. Finding solutions to the problem between exercising excessive force and the bounds of morality is an ongoing initiative for the US military's policy in the Middle East.

In any event, the precision that comes from technology and remote control alters the very definition of America's role in the region from the assurance of stability to an active participant in conflict engagement by striking with utmost efficiency, lowering danger, and shaping conflicts in their favour. With ongoing technological advances, the US needs to engage remotely with the Middle East to safeguard its interests and foster stability in the region.

The Impact on Counterterrorism Efforts

As the military adjusts its operations in the Middle East, it simultaneously enables greater regional counter-terrorism functions. While the US is readjusting its global security roles internationally, a shift towards a greater focus on technology exists. With a new focus will come new opportunities for combating extremist groups.

One of the most important factors is a movement towards more precise surveillance-based intelligence hunting. Precision killing methods that reduce collateral damage to civilians and terrorist civilians not only make defeating networks of terrorists easier but also restrict their movements far greater than before, most notably the use of drones. Drones serve a critical purpose in ventilated and unreachable regions, aiding in the defeat of terrorists, leaders, and the systems that help them function.

While the aids of technology, especially unmanned systems, enable remote violence, the action gives birth to many ethical, moral, and legal ramifications. Increasing advanced weapons as well as surveillance aid gives way to greater power from spearheading terrorists that non-state actors have, which only puts more strain on counter-terrorism tactics.

Another prominent aspect is the effect of changing military focus areas on the region's counter-terrorism partnerships. With the US adjusting its security posture, it becomes critical to ensure that allies and partner states have the will and ability to confront the root causes of extremism and enduring counter-terrorism activity. The integration of coalitions and the flow of information require constant scrutiny to maximise collaboration in responding to transnational challenges.

Moreover, the changing nature of conflict in the region requires more than just kinetic solutions; it needs an all-encompassing strategy. Responding to extremist ideology, managing socioeconomic grievances, and strengthening governance is crucial in staving off resurgence. Thus, troop deployment adjustments need to be part of a comprehensive realignment that incorporates diplomatic, developmental, and covert intelligence operations.

Considering the implications for counter-terrorism measures, recalibrating America's security role in the Middle East evaluates how deeply America engages with terrorism. The technology, the region, and their partnerships are contending elements, which, together with many strategies to counter the enduring security concern, are complicated by shifting geopolitics.

International responses and perceptions

The redefined American defence strategy in the Middle East invites scrutiny from various international stakeholders. As the US shifts its security focus within the region, global powers such as Russia and China have observed this realignment and its potential impacts on their geopolitical interests. Both nations are trying to exploit what they view as a gap in US military presence to increase their influence and expand their strategic footprint. This has created an unprecedented environment of manoeuvring competition among major powers that can have consequences beyond the Middle East.

In addition, other regional US allies, including Saudi Arabia, the UAE, and Israel, have shown support for and concern over the evolution of American defence strategies. These countries acknowledge the importance of US involvement in sustaining stability but also struggle with the unpredictability of the shift towards militaristic restraint. The challenge of formulating autonomous security strategies in conjunction with American defence policies accentuates the difficulty of formulating alliance policies in strategic recalibration.

At the same time, state and non-state actors and regional enemies have been watching closely how the ease of US military intervention changes. In particular, Iran has kept a close eye on this shift. Their leaders have carefully tried to manage the hopes of relaxed tensions while figuring out the strategic problems posed by a more reserved US role. Observing this real American shift in focus, non-state actors, including Hezbollah and Hamas, have also been recalibrating their strategies to exploit the pervasive shifts in the region's power dynamics.

The discourse of US military restraint and development has not only been limited to the immediate region. It has echoed throughout international institutions and forums, discussing the impact of world order balance and security architecture power relations. Europe, NATO, and American allies, particularly, have paid attention to the narrative of a shift in defence strategy and its impacts on transatlantic security cooperation and the global international order.

Conclusion: Forecasting the Future of American Defense Strategy

The international community's responses and views regarding the realigned US security role in the Middle East indicate a blend of interests. Seeking understanding within the context of global responses alongside an American paradigm answers the changes in American defence policy without explaining why the interests reshaping the security dynamics have become so complex in this region.

A blend of interrelated factors will affect the future of the American defence strategy for the region. The tried and tested methods of military deployment are likely to be influenced by geopolitical realignment, advancements in technology, and the necessity of having some level of military expenditure control. The idea of burden sharing among willing coalition partners appears set to emerge as a feasible approach to achieving enduring security in the region without overly straining American resources.

In addition, greater emphasis will be placed on utilising intelligence and counter-terrorism special forces, along with diplomacy, to address other ongoing asymmetric threats to national security without the need to employ large ground forces. This approach exemplifies precision and sophistication in military action, necessitating adopting new strategies tailor-made for new challenges.

American defence strategies will have to consider modern technology, especially in unmanned systems and cyber warfare. Advances in military operations, such as the use of precision munitions, expand lethality while reducing risk to personnel. Such changes mark a shift from direct and heavy striking to remote and light approaches, increasing the effectiveness of military power projection.

Furthermore, as the world progresses forward with new revolutionising sources of energy, re-balancing the fundamentals of the defence strategy requires recalibrating the consequences of energy self-sufficiency and new developing markets. While the Gulf security architecture remains very important, the injury of America's approach to friends and foes is refreshingly recalibrated – this adjustment towards energy realities is long overdue.

Insofar as American defence policy regarding the Middle East goes, strategy anticipates absolute balancing of sharp pragmatism mixed with extreme diplomacy and inventive foresight. While the United States is dealing with a multipolar world order, transnational security challenges, and straining national resources, the sustainable and efficient defence posture will rely on the careful balance between the calibrated interests, weight of responsibilities, and power projection. Achieving these objectives demands well-structured, competent policies, steadfast alliances, and a deep commitment to the firmly established notion of stability and security within the ever-changing geopolitical environment.

10

Great Power Competition

Navigating Chinese and Russian Interests

Overview of Great Power Competition in the Middle East

Throughout history, the Middle East has stood as a region of immense geopolitical importance, with its strategic location and abundant energy resources drawing the attention of major world powers. The changing global order in recent years has only served to escalate the great power competition in the region, creating intricate patterns of conflict and challenge. The transformation of the geopolitical scenario in the Middle East has been underscored by the resurgence of Russia under President Vladimir Putin, coupled with the growing economic presence and assertive foreign policy of China. Therefore, analysing the consequences of this evolving great power competition on stability, security, diplomatic relations, and the overall balance of power in the region becomes even more pertinent. The shifts in US policy aimed at re-prioritising its role in the region oddly coincide with increased Chinese and Russian interest, which creates both opportunities and challenges for the region's future. In order to grasp their current policies and plans for the Middle East, a study focused on the historical context of Russian and Chinese interests in the region is essential. It is possible to understand why and how these powers engage with the region by studying the interests established during the time of colonisation and how they have evolved to the present day.

Furthermore, studying the intertwining of historical occurrences, local power relations, and the shifts in global power gives a holistic approach to understanding the dynamics of great power competition in the Middle East. This initial chapter will set the conditions for defining the strategic goals and economic resources along with the geopolitical lenses the great powers utilise to compete in the Middle East. Only by analysing the historical roots of this rivalry can one unravel the delicate web of self-interest and self-serving motives responsible for shaping international relations today. In addition, analysing the past trajectories of China and Russia's engagement with the Middle East allows for better assessment and forecasting of plausible scenarios. While studying the dynamics of great power competition in the Middle East, it is evident that one cannot do without understanding the history of contemporary geopolitical tensions.

Historical Context: Evolution of Chinese and Russian Interests

Weaving through the Middle East's great power competition, allowing oneself to view the context of China and Russia's regional development is crucial. The Chinese presence is marked by the development of the Silk Road, which not only portrayed China's cultural and economic splendour but also China's relation to trade and further evolved with contemporary projects as China began pursuing energy resources. Forming strategic partnerships and investing in development projects helped bolster China's energy needs. As the Chinese Belt and Road Initiative projects marked the new age of economic rivalry, they further solidified China's influence in the Middle East by seeking trade relations; Russia, on the contrary, marked further resources to the Middle East because, during the Soviet era, Russia heavily focused on military support, ideological influence, and regional strategic alliances, furthering its relations even after the collapse of the Soviet Union through diplomatic ties and military cooperation.

The Syrian conflict exemplifies the way Russia began reasserting its influence in the region and is viewed as marking a turning point in Russian policy towards the Middle East. Furthermore, the international relations of these states with some of the countries in the Middle East are still informed by domestic issues, global developments, and shifts in the balance of power. Appreciating the historical context of Chinese and Russian involvement in the Middle East is not just crucial, but a prerequisite for understanding their current actions and predicting their future plans regarding the area's geopolitical environment.

China's Strategic Inroads: Economic Leverage and Soft Power

As the Middle East undergoes a realignment of geopolitical interests, China has emerged as a central actor in the region, leveraging its economic resources and soft power to significantly increase its presence. We will delve deeper into China's strategic inroads and examine how it has advanced its policies in the region by employing economic and soft power, a combination that has significantly shaped the region's dynamics.

Economic Leverage: China's Middle Eastern policy is distinguished by significant trade relations, energy cooperation, and even greater investment in infrastructure projects. China has devoted considerable financial resources to developing infrastructural projects, enhancing connectivity, and promoting regional economic development through the Belt and Road Initiative (BRI). Furthermore, China's developing appetite for the area's energy resources has strongly accelerated the formation of energy partnerships, thereby marking China as the most important economic partner in the region.

Soft Power Dynamics: In addition to the above-mentioned economic strategies, China has also focused on expanding its soft power in the region through cultural and educational exchanges and further diplomatic interactions. The establishment of the Confucius Institutes, along with other Chinese language programmes and academic scholarships, has helped to forge strong cultural connections and a positive view of China among the states in the Middle East. China has furthermore realigned its diplomatic policies to the strategic interests of countries in the region, creating friendship and further close relations.

Regional Implications: The increasing economic engagement of China in the Middle East has shifted the region's economic dependencies as trade diversification is observed and the historical reliance on Western markets is abated. In addition, the emerging and underdeveloped Chinese markets have injected much-needed investment capital that fuels infrastructure and modernisation of the region's economy. The positive effects of Chinese investments, however, pose new challenges such as debt dependency rat traps, colonial exploitation, and strategic penetrations that require attention to the impact and intentions of China.

Risk Assessments: China's growing investments in the region significantly enhance its influence, but the adoption of such manoeuvres also exposes China to new risks of political complications, socio-economic subjugation, and conflict of interest with other international players in the region. The appropriate strategy for China and regional stakeholders requires balancing capitalising on the opportunity and mitigating the risks.

Conclusion: As China expands its activities in the Middle East, it becomes crucial to highlight the fractured relations of soft power, economic power, and the power competition between China and the rest of the world concerning the region's changing geopolitics. It is important to develop approaches and strategies designed to address multifarious regional issues that protect the interests of the balance of power in the region.

Russian Military Engagements: Balancing Influence and Alliances

The Russian military has changed the geopolitical dynamics of the

Middle East region throughout history. It has strategically tried to dominate the area using relations, arms, and security pacts. Russia is known for militarily intervening in the Syrian Civil War, backing the Assad government with critical resources, which led to a definitive outcome in the contention. That degree of rivalry showed Russian willingness to back allies and fulfil its strategic warfare goals. Russia's projecting military power in Syria allowed it to showcase authority and shift its perception towards Russia as a global superpower. Russia further expanded its Mediterranean military presence by establishing a naval facility in Tartus, strengthening its foothold. Moreover, selling arms to other countries in the region, such as Egypt and Iraq, has helped shift the power balance and become Russia's alternative towards Western-aligned regimes.

Nonetheless, these military operations have encountered challenges. As to Russia's actions, both regional and international actors have been concerned about their alignment with authoritarian rule and the impact on regional order. The consequences of Russia's military undertakings from other global powers, especially the United States, have resulted in a complex scenario of competition and cooperation interwoven in rivalry. Understanding Russia's military exploits and their consequences in international relations requires great attention to detail, making Russian military actions far more sophisticated and entwined with global politics than they might appear at first glance. Analysing Russian military moves is critical for policymakers and analysts to understand the shifting situation in the Middle East and devise appropriate responses to the struggles for power in the area.

US Strategic Responses: Countering Chinese Initiatives

With the evolution of great power rivalries in the Middle East, the United States must identify and counter Chinese initiatives in the region. While China attempts to carve its economic space and assert its strategic interests through bold infrastructure projects, such as the Belt and Road Initiative, American policymakers are equally driven to design a sophisticated and purposeful counterstrategy that protects US interests and its regional allies. This challenge is complex and demands a combined approach of diplomacy, economy, and security. The United States is actively interacting with the nations in the Middle East to strengthen traditional alliances and establish new ones. This engagement aims to consolidate the US's presence as a reliable and allied nation of choice in the global competition for influence. US strategy also includes active mediation in regional disputes, strengthening institutional relationships, and cultivating a unified strategy for peace and development. Another important dimension of the US response to the Chinese aid is the improvement of economic ties. Through open and beneficial trade and investment policies, the United States seeks to avoid the debt trap that China poses, thus maintaining the independence of the regional states and countering China's economic advances.

The advocacy of fair and reciprocal trade agreements and the development of infrastructure that aligns with local requirements are the primary pillars of this context. At the same time, the military dimension of the strategic US response includes the consolidation of active defence collaborations, deepened military integration, and the transferral of modern weapon systems for the construction of arms control to allow these states to manage collective security issues regionally. This incorporates the stepped-up protection of strategic shipping channels, the fight against terrorism, the enhancement of the region's defence and stability-maintenance capabilities, and the prevention of external domination. In addition, the US aims to establish a cooperative security system that discourages one-sided aggressions or incursions and reinforces central strategic alliances aimed at mutual defence, thus creating conditions for a balanced outcome. American decision-makers must utilise a more supple approach that simultaneously employs diplomatic, economic, and military tools to effectively respond to China's actions while advancing US interests in the Middle East.

Diplomatic Disputes: The Triangular Relationship

The rivalry and competition among the United States, China, and Russia marks the diplomacy map of the Middle East. While the United States will continue to serve its role as the central power in the region, it will have to balance the intricate triangular relationship with two more dynamic global powers, each vying for its attention and territory. This is at the essence of the tripole, a fragile geopolitical wait-and-see laden with manoeuvring quads for gain and mitigation of conflicts. The strife these three powers engage in provides insight not only into the dominance of a region but also into the security and economy of the world as a whole. The effects of these struggles are more pronounced for the US, which is traditionally allied with numerous nations in the Middle East, increasing the need to respond diplomatically to the surging influence from Russia and China without straining current commitments and alliances. In contrast, China is more eager, as indicated by their rapidly expanding strategic economic enhancements and infrastructure building in the region, to secure essential supplies.

This has worried the US and its allies, including the danger of incurring debt-trap diplomacy and the ramifications for the regional balance of power. Conversely, the geopolitical arms are twirling with Russia's military actions and weapon sales, which have had mixed results for regional actors, the United States, and the region. This has fuelled long-standing suspicions and concerns about the intentions behind the deepening Russian engagements with the Middle East. Consequently, the diplomatic strife within this triad has taken the form of rivalry over regional coalitions, activity in multilateral institutions, and the articulation of the primary debates on energy security, conflict management and resolution, counterterrorism, and stability. Managing this triangular relationship involves navigating sharp diplomacy, slow, logical steps, and a rich account of the Middle East's history, culture, regions, and global politics. Relations between the United States, China, and Russia will further deepen the region's politics into international affairs and global governance.

Economic Repercussions: Oil, Trade, and Global Market Dynamics

The Middle East's economy is affected by global markets due to the significance of oil production and trade. It is closely linked to oil production and trade, both of regional and international importance. As the era of great power rivalry continues, it is essential to analyse its repercussions on the economy, more precisely, the region's energy sector. The significance of Middle Eastern oil reserves strategically determines not only the Middle East's economic prosperity but also the policies of superpowers.

As an energy resource, oil is critical in shaping world market policy. Hence, the Middle East, a leading oil-producing and exporting region, makes it an obligatory powerhouse in sustaining or weakening the global energy market. Additionally, the volatility of oil prices poses serious threats to both regional and global powers. One crucial question arises from concerns over how these shifting policies will affect already complex economic conditions, primarily focusing on the growing ambitions of China and Russia towards the region's oil resources.

Another dimension that changes, essential for the economy, is related to trading activities. The Middle Eastern trade relationship with other countries and even those participating in great power rivalry present an elaborate structure of economic interests and investments. Analysis of the shifting trade patterns reveals how the major powers' interdependent and rival economic relationships might develop.

Shifts in the global markets also require careful analysis due to their interdependent link with the activities of the Middle East. Partnerships with superpowers such as China and Russia can greatly alter the global balance of the markets and can even change the direction of trade, currency, and industrial affiliations. These interrelated shifts require practical analysis from policymakers and strategists as they try to predict how great power rivalry affects the regional and global economy.

To summarise, the relationship of oil and trade with the world markets in the Middle East reminds us of the intertwined logic of strategies and economies, which is usually overlooked. These factors do not simply construct the region's economy but have consequences on the international level, thus calling for a deep understanding of how to deal with them.

Regional Proxy Battles: Case Studies and Implications

Proxy wars are a notable part of Middle Eastern geopolitics, as many regional and global powers employ local players to further their goals. These proxy wars are not simply black-and-white conflicts. They have many interwoven elements crucial to the region's geopolitical balance. A case study of these proxy wars is Saudi Arabia and Iran's engagement in a protracted conflict of influence over Yemen, which has turned into a proxy war. Both nations support different factions of the politically unstable and war-torn region and, bit by bit, worsen the existing humanitarian catastrophe.

Another prime example is the Syrian civil war that transformed from an internal strife into a spectacular proxy war with many international countries taking part. US interests had to adapt to Russia's military actions in support of Assad's regime, Iran's support for allied militias, and the US and its allies withdrawing their support for dismantling the Assad regime, which fuelled the volatility of Syria's political landscape at the expense of the Syrian people and other countries in the region.

The Middle East remains a stage for the American foreign strategy of competing with one another through burdensome conflicts to oust one another's economic interests. These research analyses highlight the dominant engagement patterns of state and non-state entities in deepening violence and conflict in regions to garner resources, protect interests, and capture markets without concern or consideration for human lives.

These pilot case studies reveal the lasting impacts of Middle Eastern territorial proxy confrontations that accentuate the existing security risks of humanitarian crises, socio-economic prerequisites for development, and civilian survival. In addition, the emergence of proxy wars intensifies the difficulty of diplomatically resolving disrupted relations, mitigating confrontation, or reaching sustainable solutions to perennial geopolitical disputes.

While the United States navigates international competition, managing the proxy-imbued Middle East becomes strategically intricate. Balancing control and embracing integrated regional approaches becomes vital to optimally protecting American national interests and eliminating the ultra-volatile impacts of proxy wars on domestic destabilisation.

As we wrap up, the study of regional proxy conflicts starkly illustrates how external meddling influences the security dynamics of the Middle East. Solving the issues associated with proxy warfare requires a combination of diplomacy, conflict resolution, and sustained regional collaboration.

Collaborative Opportunities: Possible Areas for US Collaboration

Within the Middle East context, there are other important spaces and regions that the United States can capitalise on as areas of collaboration to build US strategic focus for developing stability and progress in the regions. One such area is cybersecurity, which offers an arena of engagement for the US and regional allies in building systems that safeguard critical infrastructure and reduce threats from state and non-state actors. Such partnerships allow for the protection and defence of digital networks through enhanced resource cooperation among US partners.

The development of renewable energy is another potential area for multidisciplinary collaboration. With the ongoing transition to renewable sources of energy, the US has an opportunity to partner with Middle Eastern countries in developing clean energy technologies and infrastructure. Through investment in regional projects, the US can strengthen energy stability and security in the region while enhancing the effectiveness of climate change resolutions.

Moreover, the healthcare sector provides the opportunity for equally meaningful collaboration. The US has the capacity to aid in the construction of modern medical facilities and research centres by providing public health education, coupled with skill training, which could promote the creation of local solutions to rising health issues. This collaboration fosters enhanced healthcare access and outcomes for local citizens while improving relations with regional governments.

Increased cooperation relating to education also has the potential to impact a wider audience. The US can boost the nurturing of ideas and talents through academic and research collaborations and scholarship programmes, creating a great pool of future leaders from different fields. Such collaborations will help develop science and technology and promote cultural understanding, forming the basis of lasting relations between the US and the Middle East.

Furthermore, resolving humanitarian issues and enhancing refugee resettlement policies is an important avenue of cooperation for the US with regional stakeholders. By providing aid and alleviating suffering through enduring solutions for displaced populations, the US can alleviate suffering in the region and foster stability.

With continuous changes in the Middle Eastern region, the US must tackle value-based opportunities in collaboration with other nations. The US boosts its regional presence through these value-based partnerships in different fields, using Middle Eastern nations.

Conclusion: Future Trajectories and Strategic Recommendations

Predictions of the Middle East are likely to be formed due to ongoing global power struggles, strategic interests, and regional conflicts. Supporting claims regarding the competition of powers in the region, a need exists to strengthen measures that protect American interests and foster regional equilibrium. The US must enhance its diplomatic relations with old and new Middle Eastern allies. Engagement in diplomacy at multilateral forums (such as the UN) and the Middle East on a multiparty basis can help prop up conflict, Oil embargo, and the arms race. Forward-looking economic policy also needs to be implemented to help bolster American power in the region.

An example of this is expanding international trade and investment relations, which would promote economic growth in the Middle Eastern region. In addition, the US should actively encourage the exchange of ideas, students, and art to help appreciate common goals that support soft power. These endeavours will aid not only in fostering strategic alignment but also in counteracting anti-Western public sentiment. Meanwhile, America needs to keep an eye on actions taken by the US's geopolitical rivals and respond appropriately to those taken with aloofness. There is a need to boost intelligence, cyber defence, and anti-terrorism to meet the needs of new fundamental threats and maintain order in the area. Deepening military relations and increasing defence support to allies has the dual purpose of constraining aggression and improving multidimensional defence integration systems. Addressing local tensions that have the potential to cause destabilisation is important to permit constructive diplomacy to mediate inclusively. Advancement of civil rights, gender equality, and human rights underscores American values while nurturing enduring peace and prosperity in the region. Fulfilling international and alliance obligations requires the US to become more proactive in mediating regional conflicts, providing humanitarian assistance, and reconstruction efforts to restore normalcy in the afflicted communities. The US can advance the Middle East's future with careful collaboration, vigilance, and principled leadership.

11

Concluding Thoughts

Prospects for Stability or Volatility?

Recapitulating Key Challenges and Opportunities

Evaluating the level of stability within a region while considering external impact factors is challenging. It has been a theme in this analysis that attempts to find a balance between domestic realities and the international environment, which is highlighted throughout the entire process. As we summarise the main challenges and opportunities in this book, it is noticeable that achieving stability in the Middle East remains fundamentally both an internal and external affair. One of the major issues remains a very deep history of conflicts and the fierce geopolitical rivalries that define the region. The changing nature of security issues, including terrorism and cyber warfare, makes searching for sustainable stability even more difficult. The complexities of interdependence within the energy and strategic resources markets bring challenges and possibilities for cooperation. The other side of the coin is the newly emerging diplomatic windows and frameworks to be ushered in by the Abraham Accords, which will change the direction of peace and conflict in the region. There is also a possibility of achieving economic diversification and eco-innovation, which may relieve the region of tensions and create prosperity. The increasing ability of the regional directorate to determine their membership to this club creates an opening for unfiltered effort.

Understanding the existence of historical wrongdoings and modern-day conflicts highlights the severity of the issues at hand. At the same time, considering the change that can stem from new policies, the economic integration of nations, and citizen diplomacy shows how lasting stability can be established. Therefore, the balance between recognising the hurdles while also capturing the openings is crucial in crafting a solution for strengthening stability within the region while facing external factors. This balanced approach is not just a strategy, but a necessity in the complex landscape of the Middle East.

Assessing Regional Stability Amidst External Influences

Internal and external considerations have always interacted regarding the balance of power and stability in the Middle East. To appreciate this region's dynamics properly, we must trace the contours of external impacts on the area. The core of global rivalry has, without exception, been the Middle East, and the geopolitical competition of world actors has and continues to worsen pre-existing cleavages and conflicts. The actions and strategies of the United States, Russia, China, Europe, and the European Union have noteworthy impacts on the region's balance.

As far as the Middle East is concerned, the United States is a pivot state. Its preoccupation with issues ranging from energy security to the promotion of democracy, balancing of power, and creation of military authoritarian systems have led to multidimensional foreign policy objectives. It has military forces and regional allies, such as Saudi Arabia, and aid policies and diplomacy support them. The set policies have both stabilising and destabilising impacts. The balance of power in the region has always been impacted by the decisions made in Washington, which, more often than not, is accompanied by tension and conflict.

Likewise, the reemergence of Russian presence within the region, specifically in Syria and arms dealings, has added fresh dimensions to the regional struggle. The strategic alliance between Russia and some local players has modified the traditional power balances and aggravated the fragility of security arrangements alongside rising proxy wars. Additionally, China's need for energy and its ongoing infrastructural endeavours in the Middle East mark the region's changing paradigm with potential strategic consequences. The country's growing investment and trade activities with other countries make it the world's largest energy consumer, which can alter the economic and security landscape of the Middle East.

In addition, the United Kingdom's foreign policy and those of other European countries towards the Middle East, in the case of Europe, migration, trade, and international counter-terrorism focus on the region's stability. The varied external factors already mentioned are responsible for forming the eastern part of the Mediterranean and the region, shaping the intricate network of

dependencies, rivalries, and alignments along with their consequences. Thus, for the Middle East and its competition with global
powers, it is essential to analyse these external factors and determine the level of external intervention needed for peace.

Analysing the Long-term Consequences of US Policies

The US policies in the Middle East have a dominant effect and
require deep analysis encompassing both intended and unintended consequences. To encompass them all, it is safe to say that
America's history and policies have greatly impacted the balance
of power and the fate of the nations. Along with this statement
comes the intricate web of complexities such as inter-state politics,
economics, and society. Mark my words; these policies will med-
dle with everything and anything. Even the most infused parts of
America will be disturbed.

The responses have been marked by great controversies, such as
socially enabled military interventions and peace attempts. Along
with this comes trade, alliances, sanctions, and participation on
a multilateral basis, which tend to solve some problems while
creating an equal number of issues. US policies in these areas
have generated enormous amounts of anger alongside scraps of
support, adding overlap to cross-cutting relations and votes. The
outcomes vary greatly for the countries in the region, making it
unstable and posing the danger of manipulating key conflicts and
grand resources. Lastly, focusing on domestic and global policies
and national interests becomes quite engaging with these complex
structures.

The policies set in the US have drastically changed the Middle

East by altering its economy, resources, and finances. Concepts like energy supremacy, commercial relationships, and even development assistance have profoundly established economic order throughout the region. In the socioeconomic context, the strategic isolation of the region has significantly impacted job opportunities, living standards, and investment trends. In tandem with the enduring isolation challenges the region strives to overcome, addressing these socio-economic legacies is essential while discerning adaptability and sustainably shaped development visions concerning infrastructural order and other accelerative factors.

The impacts of US policies can also be seen in social aspects such as culture, education, and social life. Changes in American policies have affected the sponsorship of ideas and information, including the subsequent exchange of culture. Fulbright exchanges, media, and national non-profit organisations have inspired change among hundreds of people, impacting the very core of society. However, the possible risks of cultural domination, conflict of ideas, local empowerment, ability, and heroic narratives about localisation need to be explored.

Underlying the assessment of the consequences over several years is the nuanced understanding that US policies have intricately operated within the Middle East. Understanding the region's complex historical legacies is essential in comprehending that the region's history is multifactorial, along with contemporary challenges and future opportunities. Grasping such complexities makes understanding policy design and international relations more systematic and well-balanced, thereby enhancing the focus on responsible thought and engagement that inspires action.

The Role of Local Actors: Drivers of Peace or Perpetuators of Conflict?

One must understand the local population to fully appreciate the dynamics of peaceful coexistence and conflict interactions within the Middle East. From grassroots movements to the political elite, local actors play a significant role in determining the region's focus. Some have arguably promoted animosity and power struggles, while others have pushed for coexistence and reconciliation.

Doing everything possible to prevent violence and conflict requires the emergence of diplomatic leaders who engage in peaceful negotiations for solutions. By utilising their power to resolve divides through discussions, visionaries advocate for sustainable treaties that confront historical issues. On the other hand, certain groups have proven to be a threat to peace by consolidating power through the exploitation of religion, ethnicities, and sects, which strengthens their position while destabilising society.

Civic and grassroots movements responding to social issues fall under civil society and are one of the primary features of this dichotomy. Most of these movements seem to positively ignite a shift by mobilising and uniting people around shared ideals of embracing coexistence, inclusiveness, and tolerance. Social cohesion and conflict mitigation are achieved with the purposeful cultivation of dialogue and understanding. It has been observed that the opposite, where these groups are marginalised or co-opted, leads to an absence, which fosters an environment for conflict and unrest.

Local socio-economic conditions dictate local conflict or peace. Unchecked economic competition and limited resource access may lead to social unrest and violence. Extremist ideologies can easily penetrate these vulnerable societies. On the opposite extreme, controlled violence through legal means promotes economic development because violence creates debilitating effects on societies. In this regard, investment in education and its commensurate inclusion in job creation initiatives builds social resilience.

The recall of past events and collective memory drive change, working together with the underlying narrative. Addressing different perspectives of history is one way of moving forward, acknowledging past grievances, and building sustainable empathy. Media and culture also shape public ideologies and are among the most influential bodies driving change, demonstrating the need to advocate for a peaceful narrative that aids rather than aggravates conflict.

The complexity of the region is reflected in the different roles locals assume. Forging movable agreements with these stakeholders promises sustainable change towards inclusive societies and an end to protracted conflicts.

Evaluating Prospects for Economic Growth and Cooperation

When considering the opportunities for economic growth and cooperation within the Middle East, it becomes clear that these factors are intricately connected to the region's politics and international relations. The Middle East's economy is a product of many oil dependencies, diversification attempts, and demographic shifts. Countries are putting efforts into accommodating new technologies, changing social conditions, and resolving the constraints imposed by financial and political instabilities. Regional and international stakeholders must work together towards constructive and sustainable solutions.

The Middle East's economic prospects are relatively high due to the region's young population and the available market prospects. However, achieving these prospects necessitates balancing social and economic inequalities, fostering entrepreneurship, and improving governmental systems. In addition, more economic growth and innovations would improve the region's competitiveness globally.

The cooperation of Middle Eastern states is critical for utilising shared strengths and addressing common problems. Foreign trade policies and investment agreements can lead to strengthened economic resilience and the growth of a unified market capable of attracting foreign investments. Moreover, infrastructure development initiatives, improvement of trade and transport linkages, and establishment of trade corridors can provide for the unimpeded movement of goods and services, thus contributing to the sustainable development of the region's economy.

The dynamics of globalisation present a crucial opportunity for the Middle East to rethink and reshape its economic policies to align with the emerging digital world. The region needs to adopt technologies, bolster digital infrastructure, and develop human capital to harness the benefits of the Fourth Industrial Revolution. The Middle Eastern states would greatly benefit from focusing on high-value industries, thereby positioning the region as a primary target for investment.

Creating an environment conducive to economic growth and synergy must be done without mitigating underlying geopolitical issues and chronic conflicts. The region's economic potential remains untapped without fundamental frameworks for lasting security and stability. Thus, sustaining peaceful measures to solve existing conflicts, encouraging political dialogues, and fostering trust among states is essential.

To summarise, economic development and collaboration prospects in the Middle East remain deeply connected to an integrated model featuring economic restructuring, interstate synergy, technological advancement, and peacemaking activities. While the region continues grappling with shifting geopolitical realities, opportunities like economic diversification, fostering regional mobility, and aligning policies for sustainable development will go a long way toward ensuring a prosperous future for the region.

Anticipating Shifts in Power Dynamics: A Forecast

As we move towards scanning the ever-expanding geophysical compass in the Middle East region, it becomes critical to assess and predict the possible shifts that may considerably affect the regional balance of power. This region and its traditional activities are also impacted by several other cumulative factors, including the resurgence of known global alliances such as the OPEC and the EU, competing for energy dominance, and new energy players like Qatar and the UAE. The established powers in the region, such as Saudi Arabia and Iran, are realigning their policies regarding the international system. At the same time, the heightened activity of non-state actors, from powerful multinational corporations to militant transnational extremist organisations, poses increasingly sophisticated challenges to traditional state-centred paradigms. In laying out the forecast based on those shifts, it is important to analyse the combination of national goals, ideological drives, and emerging phenomena like new technologies and environmental concerns. Additionally, the history of U.S. policy towards the region and its changes under different administrations has been a critical factor in determining power structures. The loss of American hegemony elements and mid-flywheels controlling U.S. influence pose significant shifts to the plains of dominance framework within the region.

Considering these many factors, the forecast must also integrate the primary driving forces of power about demographic changes, socio-political movements, and their associated historical grievances. The complex network of regional friendships, enmities, and rivalries also calls for a precise assessment of how these relations might change and alter the existing power structure. Economically, the elevation of certain states' capabilities and influence might emerge from the diversification of revenue intake and the increase in technology and infrastructure investment. This forecast requires an analysis of potential clashes and alignments of the regional and global order—particularly with the ongoing competition between the world's dominant and emerging powers. It is unquestioningly clear from the previous discussion that the intricate and unpredictable nature of the Middle Eastern power dynamics requires a more holistic and flexible approach to understanding and analysing them if one wishes to make any effective or sensible predictions. This approach underscores the need for adaptability and foresight in shifting power dynamics and evolving alliance structures.

Potential Risks: Instigators of Volatility

Middle Eastern risks are numerous and can profoundly impact the fragile equilibrium of power in the region. One such risk is the ongoing Israeli-Palestinian conflict, which remains a cauldron of violence and tension. The absence of a comprehensive solution poses challenges to the security and stability of the two contending parties and impacts the security of other nations in the region. The ongoing proliferation of non-state actors, such as militant and terrorist organisations, further threatens the stability of the area. Such groups frequently ignore recognised diplomatic borders and utilise available divides to complicate peaceful coexistence further. Besides, the emerging possibility of Iran becoming a nuclear power continues to be an alarming risk that could ignite a perilous arms race and an escalation in geopolitical confrontations. Civil wars in Syria and Yemen continue to prop up new humanitarian disasters while turning into new hotspots for broader regional conflicts, reinforcing the peril of additional instability.

Also, the socio-economic instability of some oil-dependent Gulf states due to long-term market changes or shifts in energy paradigms poses some risk. External geopolitical tensions and the involvement of other supra-regional actors exacerbate an already delicate situation within the region, increasing the risks of conflict escalation or miscalculation. If not solved, these issues could become significant obstacles to achieving stability in the Middle East, requiring sophisticated strategies to address potential instability.

Strategic Recommendations: Balancing Engagement with Caution

Strategic recommendations regarding Middle Eastern geopolitics require balancing area engagement and caution. First, advancing diplomacy to promote dialogue and confidence-building among regional stakeholders is critical. Such an approach will help de-escalate growing tensions and achieve stable, constructive, long-lasting peace. Furthermore, proactive involvement with essential players, long-standing allies, and new emerging powers can help align interests and foster collective action towards defined objectives. This, however, needs to be exercised with caution, as over-dependence on any single actor or alliance might cause harmful political, sociological, and economic diplomatic linkages.

Furthermore, caution involves a keen awareness of the region's societal, cultural, and historical foundations. Through actively integrating these considerations into policy-making, context-appropriate strategies can be developed. While the region faces complex problems, there is a need to delicately evaluate the risks and opportunities of engaging the region on diplomatic, economic, and military security frameworks. With shifting power dynamics and evolving alliance structures, culturally grounded credibility dictates that any recommendation focuses on how it will reverberate throughout the region.

A complete view of socio-economic advancement, climate change resilience, and human rights is essential for developing sustainable regional structures. Constructive relations based on respect, transparency, and mutual regard have been the foundation for effective engagement in the Middle East. Moreover, focusing on inclusivity and multilateralism can help build a positive and peaceful regional balance. Also, policy suggestions should be directed towards adaptive and agile approaches that respond to shifting geopolitical realities while holding firm to peace and stability. Engaging with care enables regional stakeholders to navigate towards a future of enhanced cooperation, enduring prosperity, and deepened security. Following these policy suggestions could significantly improve long-term and peaceful opportunities in the Middle East.

Long-term Vision: Ideal Outcomes for Regional Frameworks

When considering the future of the Middle East, ideal scenarios and outcomes regionally and globally need to be achieved for sustained stability. Regarding the region, many political, economic, and social factors must be considered within a single structure. The most vital is setting up inclusive and representative regional governance frameworks. This requires a comprehensive promotion of democratic environments, human rights, and participation of many different social aspects in decisions. Solving historical disputes and reconciliation is highly necessary to fulfil this order.

The long-term objectives for the Middle East will always include achieving sustainable development and prosperity. This will require diversifying economies, fostering entrepreneurship, and investing in human capital to reach the vast potential of the region's people. Moreover, strengthening cooperation and integration at the regional level will enhance the region's resistance to external shocks and provide an environment for shared development. The realisation of these objectives will rely heavily on Middle Eastern nations strategically investing in infrastructure, advanced technologies, and innovations.

Concerning security, the long-term vision aims to develop trusting relationships, cooperation, and confidence-building measures among regional actors. This involves creating effective mechanisms for resolving conflicts, demilitarising contested areas, and permanently marking peace treaties designed to stop fighting and address the fundamental causes of fighting. Focusing on self-sustaining security guarantees and enforcing arms limitation treaties helps reduce escalation tendencies and achieve lasting peace and sustainable stability.

From social and cultural perspectives, appreciation of other different cultures, the promotion of diversity, and intercultural dialogues are vital for the long-term perspective vision. Efforts to encourage acceptance, empathy, and respect for cultural diversity promote social cohesion and reduce the chances of intra-state conflicts. Education is significant in nurturing stringent global citizens and contributing to an inclusive, tolerant, and interconnected world.

In conclusion, the long-term vision for the regional frameworks in the Middle East aims to develop strong, inclusive, and prosperous societies that foster peace, cooperation, and shared development. A balanced approach and overcoming these challenges provide ideal outcomes that require collective endeavour, visionary leadership, and sustained commitment from local, regional, and international actors.

Final Reflections: A Precarious Path Towards Equilibrium

Throughout this discussion regarding the intricacies and dynamics of the Middle East, one notices rather quickly that the pursuit of equilibrium in the region is indeed a precarious path. The deep-rooted issues, such as geopolitical rivalries and historical grudges, certainly test and strain the stability of the region's ever-enduring complexities. Looking back at the previous section's long-term vision, it is clear that achieving ideal outcomes for frameworks within the region does indeed require significant amounts of effort and deliberate planning. Our aim is to encapsulate the balancing act that is the region in its search for equilibrium while navigating towards equilibrium.

Obtaining regional equilibrium means understanding the vast web of relationships between several countries. No stakeholder that seeks to resolve the issues in the region can effectively do so without engaging in cooperative dialogue with the others. Furthermore, granting representation to all of the ethnic and religious communities helps establish more robust governance and, in turn, sustainable peace, as well as fosters stability. Indeed, the people in charge cannot be ignored, as they can influence their course, enabling control over their destiny or future. By engaging them in this way, the solutions found will bear greater acceptance.

Lastly, when considering the delicate balancing axis of stability and volatility, one needs to understand the external effects that block the region locally.

Unlike global actors' blunt approach, the role of international powers, especially in shaping regional policies and alliances of smaller regions, requires nuanced attention. Such regional actors can slow or change the course of destabilisation and conflict while bidding towards constructive coexistence through careful, astute actions and diplomatic strategies. Moreover, engaging great powers proactively can unlock opportunities for constructive intervention in disputes and pursuing aligned interests.

Confronting the region's deeply ingrained disputes with honest historical revisionism is essential, though perilous, in pursuing balance. These issues require the most profound courage and a genuine will for reconciliation and empathy. Without confronting historical traumas alongside creating avenues for healing, balance will very much remain elusive. Initiatives that encourage interfaith dialogues alongside cultural and historical exchanges will foster peace and reconciliation at home. Alongside these, focusing on children with educational programmes that promote tolerance and diversity will pivot the region towards enduring peace and stability.

In the Middle East, particular integrated geographic areas containing core countries govern multifaceted relations of utmost importance. Therefore, forming solid diplomatic and trade relations and even security cooperation agreements between regional actors will provide a firm foundation of trust and a strong framework for collaboration. If shared and collective economic augments are adopted, it will be easier for the concerned parties to achieve smooth synergies and sustainable development.

About the tentative path towards equilibrium balance, I want to highlight again the need and importance of far-sighted leaders. Compared with others, far-sighted leaders are defined by knowing how to deal with complex issues, foresee scenarios in which good things can happen, and have the boldness needed to implement the required changes. Such leaders are the ones who embrace clear-sighted thinking and practice humanitarian policies based on social justice, equity, and comprehensive inclusion of all forms of identities. Their commitment to working for the good of peaceful coexistence will be, in the eyes of all, a sorely needed support in the storms that will, without doubt, ravage the area. While engaged with such deep thoughts, I hope that we nurture hope, resolve, and optimism, together with the determination to look for justice in the Middle East, which is a great challenge caused by all of us endlessly.

Selected Bibliography

Books

1. Alterman, J. B. (2020). *The long shadow of Trump: America's global role after the storm*. Columbia University Press.
2. Ben-Meir, A. (2021). *Trump and the Middle East: The legacy of chaos*. Palgrave Macmillan.
3. Blumenthal, M. (2020). *The management of chaos: Donald Trump and the Middle East*. Verso Books.
4. Bogle, J. (2021). *Trump's foreign policy: America first or America alone?* Routledge.
5. Brooks, R. (2020). *The great disruption: Trump and the Middle East*. I.B. Tauris.
6. Cohen, E. A. (2021). *Trump's world: The consequences of a chaotic presidency*. Columbia University Press.
7. Cordesman, A. H. (2019). *Trump and the Middle East: From bad to worse*. Rowman & Littlefield.
8. Drezner, D. W. (2020). *The ideas industry: How pessimists, partisans, and plutocrats are transforming the marketplace of

ideas*. Oxford University Press.

9. Entous, A., & Rosenbach, M. (2021). *The shadow war: Iran's revenge and the perilous future of the Middle East*. PublicAffairs.

10. Fisk, R. (2021). *The great war for civilisation: The conquest of the Middle East*. Vintage.

11. Freedman, L. (2020). *The future of war: A history*. PublicAffairs.

12. Gause, F. G. (2020). *The international relations of the Persian Gulf*. Cambridge University Press.

13. Goldberg, J. (2021). *Trump's foreign policy: Reckless or revolutionary?* Brookings Institution Press.

14. Gordon, M. R. (2020). *Dethroning the Saudis: America and the new global energy economy*. John Wiley & Sons.

15. Harris, D. (2021). *The enigma of Donald Trump: An insider's perspective*. Oxford University Press.

16. Henderson, S. (2020). *Trump and the Middle East: The first three years*. The Washington Institute.

17. Hopkins, M. (2021). *The Trump effect: The president's impact on American foreign policy*. Cambridge University Press.

18. Indyk, M. (2020). *Master of the game: Henry Kissinger and the art of Middle East diplomacy*. Knopf.

19. Jones, S. G. (2021). *The mirage of security: U.S. grand strategy in the Middle East*. Cornell University Press.

20. Katzman, K. (2020). *U.S. policy toward the Persian Gulf monarchies*. Congressional Research Service.

21. Kupchan, C. A. (2020). *Isolationism: A history of America's efforts to shield itself from the world*. Oxford University Press.

22. Laron, G. (2021). *The state of the Middle East: An atlas of conflict and resolution*. University of California Press.

23. Mandelbaum, M. (2020). *The rise and fall of peace on earth*. Oxford University Press.

24. Miller, A. (2022). *The Arab Winter: A tragedy*. Hutchinson.

25. Nye, J. S. (2021). *Do morals matter? Presidents and foreign policy from FDR to Trump*. Oxford University Press.

26. O'Sullivan, N. (2020). *The globalist delusion: How the elite undermines democracy and drives globalization*. Bloomsbury Publishing.

27. Rabinowitz, A. (2021). *The lingering crisis: The Middle East and U.S. policy*. Hoover Institution Press.

28. Rubin, M. (2020). *Trump and the Middle East: From disruption to strategy*. The Washington Institute.

29. Sanger, D. E. (2021). *The perfect weapon: War, sabotage, and fear in the cyber age*. Crown Publishing Group.

30. Walt, S. M. (2020). *The hell of good intentions: America's foreign policy elite and the decline of U.S. primacy*. Farrar, Straus and Giroux.

Miscellaneous sources and references

1. "The abraham accords declaration." *International Legal Materials*, vol. 60, no. 3, 2021, pp. 452–452.

2. Abrams, Elliott. "Trump the Traditionalist: A Surprisingly Standard Foreign Policy." *Foreign Affairs*, vol. 96, no. 4, 2017, pp. 10–16.

3. Amidror, Yaakov. Begin-Sadat Center for Strategic Studies, 2016, *The US Must Bolster Its Global Credibility*.

4. Asan Institute for Policy Studies.(2024). *Trump's return and U.S. policy toward the Middle East in 2025*.

5. Asan Institute for Policy Studies, 2021, pp. 93–101, *Exploring the Middle East's Shifting Alignments and Rebuilding Order.*

6. Ben-Shabbat, Meir, and David Aaronson. Institute for National Security Studies, 2022, *Impressive Progress, Multiple Challenges, and Promising Potential.*

7. Biscop, Sven. Egmont Institute, 2020, *Just Leave Just Leave Things to the Proxies?*

8. Biscop, S., & Gromyko, A. (2020). *Views from the United States, China, Russia, and the European Union*. Egmont Institute.

9. Burke, Ryan, and Jahara Matisek. "The Illogical Logic of American Entanglement in the Middle East." *Journal of Strategic Security*, vol. 13, no. 1, 2020, pp. 1–25

10. Chaziza, Mordechai. Begin-Sadat Center for Strategic Studies, 2020, *Coronavirus, China, and the Middle East.*

11. Clarke, Richard A. "The US and the Middle East." *Middle East Journal*, vol. 71, no. 1, 2017, pp. 147–154.

12. Daalder, Ivo, and James M. Lindsay. "Trump's Winner-take-all Worldview." *Horizons: Journal of International Relations and Sustainable Development*, no. 14, 2019, pp. 32–57.

13. Duran, BURHANETTİN. "Türkiye and the Future of Normalization in the Middle East." *Insight Turkey*, vol. 24, no. 2, 2022, pp. 161–180.

14. Economy, E. (2019). The U.S. Rethink and Reset on China. *Horizons: Journal of International Relations and Sustainable Development, 13*, 40–51. https://www.jstor.org/stable/48573768

15. Egel, Daniel, et al. RAND Corporation, 2021, *Widening the Economic Growth and Development Benefits of the Abraham Accords.*

16. Eran, O. (2016). *The American conundrums in the Middle East, as reflected in the Clinton-Trump debate*. Institute for National Security Studies.

17. Eran, O., & Alterman, O. (2016). *The establishment, the populists, and what they mean for Israel*. Institute for National Security Studies.

18. ERDOĞAN, Ayfer, and Lourdes Habash. "Continuity or Change?" *Insight Turkey*, vol. 22, no. 1, 2020, pp. 125–146.

19. Even, Shmuel, et al. Institute for National Security Studies, 2020, *The Economic-Strategic Dimension of the Abraham Accords.*

20. Feierstein, G. M. (2018). *Policy lacks strategic coherence despite rhetoric*. Middle East Institute.

21. Galbreath, Megan. "An analysis of donald trump and ma-

rine le pen." *Harvard International Review*, vol. 38, no. 3, 2017.

22. Ghafar, Adel Abdel. Istituto Affari Internazionali (IAI), 2021, *The Growing Role of Gulf States in the Eastern Mediterranean*.

23. Guzansky, Yoel, et al. Institute for National Security Studies, 2021, *Relations between Saudi Arabia and UAE*.

24. Guzansky, Yoel. Institute for National Security Studies, 2020, *Saudi Arabia and Normalization with Israel*.

25. Guzansky, Yoel. Institute for National Security Studies, 2022, *Normalization at a Snail's Pace*.

26. GÜNEY, NURŞİN ATEŞOĞLU, and VİŞNE Korkmaz. "What the Abraham Accords Mean for Mediterranean Geopolitics and Turkey." *Insight Turkey*, vol. 23, no. 1, 2021, pp. 61–76.

27. Haar, Roberta. "How will foreign policy change after the 2016 elections?" *Atlantisch Perspectief*, vol. 40, no. 5, 2016, pp. 4–9.

28. Hamdi, Osama Anter. "Strategic Transformations." *Insight Turkey*, vol. 20, no. 2, 2018, pp. 251–272.

29. Haruko, Wada. S. Rajaratnam School of International Studies, 2020, *Geographical Adjustments and Their Implications*.

30. Hassan, Zaha, et al. Carnegie Endowment for Interna-

tional Peace, 2021, *Breaking the Israel-Palestine Status Quo*.

31. Hochschild, Arlie Russell. "The Ecstatic Edge of Politics: Sociology and Donald Trump." *Contemporary Sociology*, vol. 45, no. 6, 2016, pp. 683–689.

32. Hu, Weixing, and Weizhan Meng. "The US Indo-Pacific Strategy and China's Response." *China Review*, vol. 20, no. 3, 2020, pp. 143–176.

33. Ji-Hyang, Jang, and Park Hyondo. Asan Institute for Policy Studies, 2021, *The 2021 Iranian Presidential Election and Its Aftermath*.

34. Ji-Hyang, Jang. Asan Institute for Policy Studies, 2021, *Democratic Aspirations and Strategic Realignment in Biden's Middle East Policy*.

35. Ji-Hyang, Jang. Asan Institute for Policy Studies, 2022, *Deepening UAE-Israel Strategic Cooperation after the Abraham Accords*.

36. Ji-Hyang, Jang. Asan Institute for Policy Studies, 2024, *Trump's Return and U.S. Policy Toward the Middle East in 2025*.

37. Katulis, B., & Masthoff, A.(2024). *Comparing Harris and Trump on Middle East policy*. Middle East Institute.

38. Khalilzad, Zalmay. "Trump and a Bipartisan Foreign Policy." *The National Interest*, no. 147, 2017, pp. 79–90.

39. Krieg, A.(2017). 'Barking dogs seldom bite.' *Insight Turkey, 19*(3), 139–158. https://doi.org/10.1017/S13 05777X00001234

40. Kroenig, Matthew. "The Case for Trump's Foreign Policy: The Right People, the Right Positions." *Foreign Affairs*, vol. 96, no. 3, 2017, pp. 30–34.

41. Lee, Michael J. "Considering Political Identity: Conservatives, Republicans, and Donald Trump." *Rhetoric and Public Affairs*, vol. 20, no. 4, 2017, pp. 719–730.

42. Lo, B.(2018). *The foreign policy of Vladimir Putin*. Lowy Institute for International Policy.

43. Lucentini, Mauro. "The outlook for US foreign policy under President Donald J. Trump." *Rivista Di Studi Politici Internazionali*, vol. 83, no. 4 (332), 2016, pp. 577–588.

44. Mahmood, Nazish, and Pervaiz Iqbal Cheema. "Trump and the US Foreign Policy Crisis." *Strategic Studies*, vol. 38, no. 4, 2018, pp. 1–18.

45. Michael, Kobi, and Yoel Guzansky. Institute for National Security Studies, 2020, *Might Qatar Join the Abraham Accords?*

46. Mizrahi, Orna. Institute for National Security Studies, 2020, *Is a Strategic Change in Lebanon-Israel Relations Possible at the Present Time?*

47. Niva, S. (2017). Trump's drone surge: Outsourcing the

war machine. *Middle East Report, no. 283, 2017, pp. 2–8.

48. Pavia, Alissa, et al. Atlantic Council, 2022, pp. 29–39, *Crisis in the Maghreb.*

49. Pillar, P. R. (2017). Trump and the Middle East. *The National Interest, no. 147, 2017, pp. 49–57. https://doi .org/10.2307/26557364

50. Propper, Eyal. Institute for National Security Studies, 2020, *Israel-China Relations and the Normalization Agreements with the Gulf States.*

51. Rabinovich, Itamar. "Trump's Early Steps in the Middle East." *Horizons: Journal of International Relations and Sustainable Development*, no. 9, 2017, pp. 22–33.

52. Reveron, Derek S., and Nikolas K. Gvosdev. "An Emerging Trump Doctrine?" *Horizons: Journal of International Relations and Sustainable Development*, no. 9, 2017, pp. 42–61.

53. Saab, Bilal Y. Middle East Institute, 2021, *The Roadblocks to a Regional Security Dialogue in the Middle East.*

54. Sloan, Stanley R. "Biden or Trump and the rest of the world." *Atlantisch Perspectief*, vol. 44, no. 5, 2020, pp. 38–43.

55. Smith, Sheila A. "U.S.-Japan Relations in a Trump Administration." *Asia Policy*, no. 23, 2017, pp. 13–20.

56. Stein, Shimon, and Oded Eran. Institute for National Security Studies, 2021, *Transatlantic Cooperation and the Implications for Israel.*

57. Sutter, Robert. "Barack Obama, Xi Jinping and Donald Trump—Pragmatism Fails as U.S.-China Differences Rise in Prominence." *American Journal of Chinese Studies*, vol. 24, no. 2, 2017, pp. 69–85.

58. Syed, Shabana, and Zainab Ahmed. "Abraham Accords, Indo-Pacific Accord and the US-Led Nexus of Curtailment: Threat to Regional Security, and Joint Counter Strategy." *Policy Perspectives*, vol. 18, no. 1, 2021, pp. 25–52, https://doi.org/10.13169/polipers.18.1.0025.

59. Trigano, Shmuel. Begin-Sadat Center for Strategic Studies, 2021, *Contrasting Reflections.*

60. Van Zoonen, D. (2016). *Four key issues*. Middle East Research Institute.

61. Winter, Ofir, and Yoel Guzansky. Institute for National Security Studies, 2020, *Religious Aspects of the Abraham Accord.*

62. Woon, W. (2021). From trade war to race and culture confrontation. *Prism*, vol. 9, no. 2, 2021, pp. 46–57.

63. "The world in brief." *The World Today*, vol. 73, no. 5, 2017, pp. 5–8.

64. Wright, T. (2016). *The 2016 presidential campaign and the crisis of US foreign policy*. Lowy Institute for Inter-

national Policy.

65. Wright, T. (2020). *The 2020 election and the crisis of American foreign policy*. Lowy Institute for International Policy.

66. Ya'alon, Moshe. Institute for National Security Studies, 2016, *Policy Recommendations on the Middle East for the Trump Administration*.

67. Zakheim, Dov S. "Can Trump Take Advice?" *Horizons: Journal of International Relations and Sustainable Development*, no. 15, 2020, pp. 206–219.

68. Zakheim, Dov S. "The Case Against Donald Trump." *The National Interest*, no. 169, 2020, pp. 15–20.

www.ingramcontent.com/pod-product-compliance
Lightning Source LLC
Chambersburg PA
CBHW031152020426
42333CB00013B/627